IN THE SHADOW OF THE MOONS

IN THE SHADOW OF
THE M○○NS

MY LIFE IN THE REVEREND SUN MYUNG MOON'S FAMILY

NANSOOK HONG

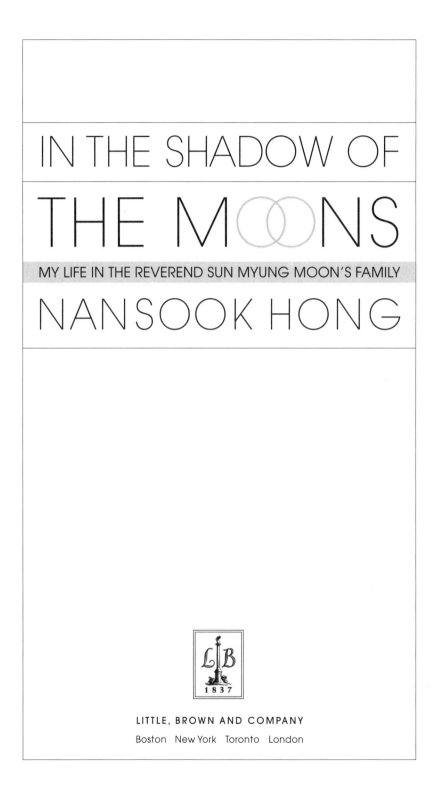

LITTLE, BROWN AND COMPANY

Boston   New York   Toronto   London

For my children

First Edition

Author's note: This is a true story. The names of Shin June, Je Jin, and Jin are fictitious in this book in order to preserve the anonymity of these family members.

ISBN 0-316-34816-3
Library of Congress Catalog
Card Number 98-66869

10 9 8 7 6 5 4 3 2

MV-NY

Published simultaneously in Canada by Little, Brown & Company (Canada) Limited

Printed in the United States of America

IN THE SHADOW OF THE MOONS

Prologue

The bleating of my beeper snapped me awake. I realized in a panic that the sun was already up. Light, streaming through the bay windows, played on the blue striped wallpaper of my baby's nursery. I could see the outline of the hills outside from the floor at the foot of Shin Hoon's crib, where I must have fallen asleep just before August 8, 1995, dawned.

I knew it was Madelene trying to reach me. A quick glance at my watch confirmed that I was late for our prearranged 5:00 A.M. rendezvous. How could I have been so careless on this of all days? After months of secret meetings and cautious planning, had I jeopardized everything at the last minute?

I stole across the wide corridor to the master bedroom, my naked feet silent on the crimson carpet. I was barely breathing as I pressed my ear to the dark lacquered door. I heard only the guttural cough that always punctuated my husband's all-night cocaine sessions.

Our only hope was that Hyo Jin's high would render him oblivious for one more morning. For months he had barely noticed as furniture, clothing, and toys disappeared from the second floor of the brick mansion where we lived on the estate of his father, the Reverend Sun Myung Moon, founder of the Unification Church and self-proclaimed Lord of the Second Advent.

It was only a week ago that Hyo Jin's bloodshot eyes had registered the absence of the IBM computer that usually occupied a corner of Shin June's room. "Where's the computer?" he'd asked Shin June, the oldest of our five children. At twelve, she fell all too naturally into the role of coconspirator. Living in the Moon compound — an atmosphere suffused less with spirituality than with palace intrigue — had taught all my children well how to keep secrets.

"It's broken, Appa; it's out being repaired," she replied without hesitation. Her father just shrugged and returned to his room.

I say "his" room because I had long since abandoned the master suite. It was less a bedroom than my husband's private drug den, its cream-colored carpet littered with cigarette butts and empty tequila bottles, its VCR programmed to play an endless assortment of pornographic videotapes.

I had tried to stay as far away as possible from that room since the previous fall, when I had discovered Hyo Jin snorting cocaine there after so many of his false promises to stop. I tried to flush the cocaine down the toilet. He beat me so severely I thought he would kill the baby in my womb. He made me sweep up the spilled white powder from the bathroom floor even as he continued to punch me. Later Hyo Jin would offer a religious justification for beating half senseless a woman seven months pregnant: he was teaching me to be humble in the presence of the son of the Messiah.

The eighteen-acre secluded compound where we lived in Irvington, forty minutes north of New York City, is the world headquarters of the Unification Church and the home of the founder of the religious movement the world knows as "Moonies." The estate, called East Garden, had been my personal prison for fourteen years, since the day the Reverend Moon summoned me from Korea to be the child bride of his eldest son, the heir to Moon's divine mission and earthly empire. Then I was only fifteen, a naive schoolgirl eager to serve her God. Now I was twenty-nine, a woman ready to reclaim her life. Today I would escape. I would take the only thing holy about this marriage, my children, and leave behind the man who beat me and the false Messiah who let him, men so flawed that I now knew that God would never have chosen Sun Myung Moon or his son to be his agents on earth.

It is easy for those outside the Unification Church to scoff at the idea that anyone would have believed such a thing in the first place. To most of the world, the name Moonies conjures up images of brainwashed young people squandering their lives hawking flowers on street corners to enrich the clever and charismatic leader of a religious cult.

There is some truth in that view, but it is much too simplistic. I was born to my faith. Just as children of more mainstream Christian religions are reared to believe that Jesus Christ is the Son of God, sent to earth to redeem the sins of mankind, I was taught in Sunday school that the Reverend Moon had been chosen by God to complete Jesus' mission to restore the Garden of Eden. The Reverend Moon was the Second Coming.

With his wife, the Reverend Moon would sire the first sinless True Family of God. His children, the True Children, would build on that flawless foundation. Members of the Unification Church would be grafted onto the True Family's pureblood lineage in wedding ceremonies arranged and blessed by the Reverend Moon, the mass nature of which has attracted so much attention around the world.

Those beliefs, isolated from the theology in which they are embedded and the culture from which they sprang, admittedly sound bizarre. But what of the miracles of Jesus? Or the parting of the Red Sea? Are Bible stories of virgin births and resurrection not equally fantastic? All belief is a matter of faith. If mine was different, it was perhaps so only in its intensity. Is there any faith more powerful, more innocent, than the faith of a child?

But all faith is tested by experience. The Reverend Moon, sinless? The Moon children, flawless? Father — who demonstrated contempt for civil law every time he accepted a paper bag full of untraceable, undeclared cash collected from true believers? Mother — who spent so much time at chic clothing emporiums that her youngest son once answered, "She shops," when his schoolteacher asked him to describe his mother's life-work? The eldest son — who smokes, drives drunk, abuses drugs, and engaged in premarital and extramarital sex, in violation of church doctrine? This family is the Holy Family? It is a myth that can be sustained only from a distance.

Accepting the Reverend Moon for the fraud I now know him to be was a slow and painful process. It was only possible because that realization, in the end, did not shake my faith in God. Moon had failed God, as he has failed me and all his idealistic and trusting followers. But God had not failed me. It was to God that I turned in loneliness and despair, a teenager on my knees in a strange house in a foreign land praying for succor. It was God alone who comforted me, a woman-child in the hands of a husband who treated me either as a toy for his sexual pleasure or as an outlet for his violent rages.

God was guiding me now as I surveyed my sleeping children and the suitcases we had been packing clandestinely for weeks. My belief in Sun Myung Moon had been at the center of my life for twenty-nine years, but a shattered faith is no match for a mother's love. My children had been my sole source of joy in the cloistered, poisonous world of the True Family. I had to flee for their sake, as well as my own.

When I first told the older ones that I would be leaving, not one chose to stay behind, despite what they knew would be the end of the lavish lifestyle they had always enjoyed. There would be no mansion, no chauffeurs, no Olympic-sized swimming pool, no private bowling alley, no horseback riding lessons, no private schools, Japanese tutors, or first-class vacations where we were going.

Outside the walls of the Moon compound, they would not be worshiped as the True Children of the Messiah. There would be no adoring church members to bow down to them and compete for the chance to serve them.

"We just want to live in a little house with you, Mama," the oldest told me, her humble fantasy mirroring my own.

And yet doubt and unanticipated sadness had kept sleep at bay for most of the night. Long after the household fell silent, I paced the halls and familiar rooms of the mansion, praying and weeping softly. Each time I had closed my eyes, my mind had filled with the questions that had haunted me for months. Was I doing the right thing? Was leaving truly a manifestation of God's will or was it a sign of my own failure? Why had I been unable to make my husband love me? Why had I been unable to change him? Should I stay and pray that my son, once grown, might one day return the Unification Church to a righteous path?

I had even more pressing fears. Leaving the orbit of the Reverend Sun Myung Moon would render me and my children spiritual outcasts, but would it put us in physical danger, too? If I fled, would the church track me down to silence me? But if I stayed would I be any safer? How many times had Hyo Jin threatened to kill me and the children? If he was high enough on drugs or booze, I knew, he was capable of making good on those threats. He certainly had the guns to do it, a veritable arsenal purchased with church funds that he used to terrorize me and anyone else who got in his way.

I reminded myself that I was not acting hastily. I had been planning for this day since the previous winter when Hyo Jin's latest, most blatant infidelity roused even the Reverend Moon from his usual indifference. When Father continued to insist that it was I who was to blame for my husband's sins, that it was my failure as a wife that accounted for his son's wayward path, I knew I had to go.

I had taken every precaution. I began to save money as soon as I made the decision to flee. I withdrew money from the bank that I had set aside for the children's education. I held on to every dollar of the thousands in cash Mrs. Moon would peri- odically hand me for spending money; when she took me to a Jaeger boutique to outfit me for the church ceremony honoring the birth of my baby, I wore the thousand-dollar outfit she purchased with the price tags discreetly tucked out of sight. I returned the clothes for a cash refund the next day.

With the help of my brother and his wife, the eldest daugh- ter of the Reverend Moon, I found a modest house in the Mas- sachusetts town where they already lived in exile from the Moons. I had been envious when they first left the church, and now here I was, a few short years later, relying on them to lead me to the freedom they'd found. I had worried for them just as I had worried for my own parents, members of the elite group of Moon's original Korean disciples, who had abandoned the Unification Church in disgust around the same time. My par- ents were waiting in Korea for word from my brother that I was free.

I was so very grateful. Too often I took my brother's support for granted, even as a child. Even when we disagreed — and we often did — Jin was always there for me. Jin found lawyers to advise me how to protect myself and my children once we were free. Their counsel helped pinpoint the day we would leave. We would flee on a Tuesday because the family court in the Massachusetts county where we would live heard requests from battered women for restraining orders against their abusive partners on Wednesdays.

I tried, too, to protect those I would be leaving behind. Kumiko had been my baby-sitter for five years. She was a devout member of the church from Japan, as was her husband, a gardener on the East Garden estate. For weeks she had watched me pack boxes, but she said nothing. No member would be impertinent enough to question one of the True Family. But for years she had seen the pain in my life firsthand. I worried that she would be called to account when the Reverend Moon learned that we were gone.

A month before we were to flee, I asked Kumiko where she and her husband would most like to live in the world. They wanted to return to Japan, to her husband's parents. They were aged and he was an only child. They wanted to go home to care for their elders.

I knew that no personnel changes happened in East Garden without the approval of Mrs. Moon, or Mother, as we addressed her. Twenty-three years younger than the aging Reverend Moon, she is increasingly the power behind the throne. We had never been close, in part because she surrounded herself with influence-hungry sycophants who elevated their own standing by reporting my perceived failures as a wife or mother. Still, long years of experience had taught me how to coax small favors from Mother.

I found myself embellishing the story as I went along. Kumiko's husband's parents were not only old in my account, they were ailing. The couple needed to return to Japan to tend to them. I would rather do without a baby-sitter than hold them from their duty. That last point would strike a chord, I knew, with Mother. How often had Father complained that his staff was too large, too expensive to feed and house? One less baby-sitter and one less gardener would be a feather in Mother's cap. She willingly agreed to let them go, telling me to be certain that Peter Kim, the Reverend Moon's personal assistant, gave them money for the trip. They flew to Japan two days before we fled.

Another young woman who helped me care for the baby was due to be married soon at home in Korea to a security guard at East Garden. I told her to extend her visit home until October, time enough, I hoped, to put some distance between our flight and her return.

Ever since the Reverend Moon had built himself a separate, twenty-four-million-dollar house and conference center on the grounds, we had shared the common areas of the nineteen-room mansion in East Garden with Hyo Jin's sister In Jin and her family. As luck — or God's design — would have it, they had gone away the weekend before and had yet to return. Even if In Jin had been alerted that I might be planning to leave, she would never have taken it seriously. Maybe I was trying to scare Hyo Jin into behaving by taking the children away, she would think. Maybe I was trying to teach him a lesson. I would be back. Neither In Jin nor anyone else in the Moon family would have believed that I would leave for good.

The truth is that not one of them knew me well enough to know what I would do. None of them knew me at all. In fourteen years in the heart of the Moon family, no one had asked me what I thought or felt about anything. They ordered; I obeyed. Today I would turn their ignorance to my advantage.

Quietly I roused Shin Hoon. He was nine months old this very morning and such a good baby; he did not cry as I dressed him in a short-sleeved jumper and then gently shook his siblings awake. I cautioned the children to dress silently while I went to meet Madelene.

In the last year, Madelene Pretorius had become my first real friend. Now, at the other end of my beeper, she was an instrument of my escape. Madelene had been lured into the Unification Church ten years earlier during a chance meeting with a Moonie on a fish pier while vacationing in San Francisco. It is a classic church recruitment technique, befriending a young person traveling alone far from home. The conversation is soon steered from pleasantries to philosophy to the church. A successful encounter ends with the tourist agreeing to attend a lecture or meeting. Some of them never go home.

For the last three years, Madelene had worked for Hyo Jin at Manhattan Center Studios, the recording facility the church owned in New York City. She had seen my husband's cocaine abuse and raging temper firsthand. When I confided my plan to flee, she had offered her help. It was risky. If he knew she had helped, he would turn on her, too.

Hyo Jin was already suspicious of our friendship. Only weeks ago he had come into the kitchen to find us talking quietly over cups of tea. He ordered me upstairs and Madelene out of East Garden. Upstairs, he threatened to break every one of my fingers if I dared to pursue a personal friendship with a church member. Such threats were typical of his controlling and possessive behavior.

I shivered now at that memory of my husband's efforts to control me. I waved at the gardener and the security guards as I drove alone through the iron gates of East Garden to meet my friend. She was waiting in front of the local deli. I would spirit her back into the compound just as I had been spiriting our belongings out of the estate for weeks. Almost daily, I made my way past the omnipresent security cameras with chairs and lamps, boxes and suitcases. The guards had accepted without question that I was just rearranging furniture and storing old clothes at Belvedere, another Moon mansion down the road. Mrs. Moon did it all the time.

In truth, I had been headed into town to the storage room I had rented to hold the furnishings of a new life. Today it was time for us to go, too. My brother and Madelene were waiting.

The streets of Irvington and Tarrytown were quiet. It was high summer, when tourists in search of the spirit of Washington Irving's Sleepy Hollow share the countryside with the locals. But it was too early for either to be stirring. I met Madelene on the designated street corner and smuggled her back into the compound under a blanket so she could help me with the children. We would return to this same corner to retrieve her car, rendezvous with my brother, and travel together to Massachusetts in a caravan.

Once we had loaded the last of the suitcases into the van, Madelene and I led five barefoot children on tiptoe past the master bedroom, down the central staircase, and out the front door. Their father never stirred.

Madelene tucked each child into any available crevice in the overloaded van and then slid into the passenger seat, careful to use blankets to conceal the children and herself from view. I eased the van slowly down the long winding driveway, lined with ancient elms, and out the front gate, smiling at a security guard who had taken his post only a few days before. I turned out of East Garden onto Sunnyside Lane. I did not look back.

1

The Reverend Sun Myung Moon is a small, compact man with thinning gray hair that he dyes a shoe-polish shade of black. If you passed him on a street in Seoul, you would not notice him, his physical appearance is so nondescript.

He is an electrical engineer by training. His speaking style is notable more for his endurance — he can drone on for hours in Korean — than for his charisma. When he preaches in English, he is barely comprehensible, eliciting unintended laughter on those frequent occasions when he fractures the language.

How, then, did this seventy-eight-year-old farmer's son emerge as the leader of a religious movement that has ensnared millions of people around the world and enriched itself with the fruit of their labors? The answer has as much to do with the time and place in which the Unification Church emerged as it does with the man himself.

The messianic message of the Reverend Sun Myung Moon might have sounded like the ravings of a madman had it been delivered on a soapbox in New York's Times Square, but the

Reverend Moon sprang from Korean soil, out of the particular circumstances of my country's spiritual traditions and its turbulent century of foreign occupation, civil war, and political division.

Korea is a land defined by its geography, a peninsula at once attached to and divided from the east Asian mainland by the Everwhite Mountains and the Yalu and Tumen Rivers. Those natural barriers kept my homeland isolated for centuries from the outside world, just as its twenty-six highest mountain peaks kept our people separated from one another. That we managed to forge a national identity and a mutual language is something of a miracle.

When foreign influence did infiltrate Korea, it came from China through the mountain passes of the north and from Japan, whose largest island, Honshu, lies only 120 miles to the east in the Sea of Japan. Because of Korea's strategic location, its history has been likened to a shrimp buffeted in the battles of whales. Outsiders eager to exploit its seaports and natural resources brought their commerce and their cultures to Korea — and, too often, their guns. They also brought their religions.

The native religion of Korea is a sort of primal shamanism. Shamans, or *mudangs,* as we call them, are believed to have special powers to commune with the spirit world. They tell fortunes and petition the spirits for blessings, such as a bountiful harvest, or relief from suffering, such as illness. They also commune with the spirits believed to inhabit the forests and mountains, and individual trees and rocks.

When the Chinese introduced Buddhism to Korea in the fourth century, this folklore did not disappear or formalize itself into a distinct religion like Taoism in China or Shintoism in Japan. Koreans merely grafted our ancient beliefs onto Buddhist teachings, which remained the dominant religious influence in Korea until the fourteenth century. Similarly, when Confucianism rose to command a prominent place in religious life for the next five hundred years, it did so alongside that folk tradition, not in place of it.

That process of incorporating native beliefs into other religious doctrines continued in the nineteenth century when Buddhism experienced a resurgence and Christianity was introduced into Korea. Even today, when Christianity is the fastest-growing religion in a still predominately Buddhist country, folklore continues to exert a powerful hold on the imagination of even the most modern Koreans. A Christian who attends church services on Sunday morning might also make an offering to the house god in the afternoon and see no inconsistency.

In addition to ancient beliefs in ancestor worship and the spirit world, there is a strong messianic strain in my culture. The notion that the Messiah or Herald of the Righteous Way would appear in Korea predates the introduction of Christianity into Korea a hundred years ago. It has its roots in the Buddhist notion of Maitreya and the Confucian idea of Jin-In, or the True Man, and in Korean books of prophecy, such as the *Chung Gam Nok*.

Likewise, the notion of kings ruling by divine right appears in the country's earliest legends. As children we all learn the ancient Korean folktale the myth of Tangun. Tangun was the son of the divine spirit Hwan-Ung, who was himself the son of the Lord of Heaven, Hwan-in. According to legend, Hwan-in granted his son permission to descend from Heaven and establish the Kingdom of Heaven on Earth. Hwan-Ung came to Korea. There he met a tiger and a she-bear who asked him how they could become human. Hwan-Ung gave them sacred food to eat. The bear obeyed and was transformed into a woman. The tiger did not obey and was forced to remain a beast. Hwan-Ung married the woman, and Tangun was born of this union of a divine spirit and a former she-bear. Tangun established his royal residence in Pyongyang and named his kingdom on earth Choson.

It was in this fertile soil that the messianic ideas of the Reverend Sun Myung Moon took root in the second half of the twentieth century. How much of his official biography is historically accurate and how much manufactured myth is a question I never asked as a child. I absorbed the story of the Reverend Moon in the same way rice absorbs water. From birth I was taught that he was not just a holy man, or a prophet. He was anointed by God. He was the Lord of the Second Advent, the divine guide who would unite the world's religions under his leadership and establish the Kingdom of Heaven on Earth. Denunciations of him by mainstream religions as a cult leader were akin to the persecution of Jesus, whose mission the Reverend Moon was divinely inspired to complete.

The Reverend Sun Myung Moon was born Young Myung Moon in a rural village of North P'yongan province in northwest Korea, three miles from the coast, on January 6, 1920, the fifth of eight children. His birth name translates as Shining Dragon. This became a problem later in life. Because the dragon is a symbol of Satan, he changed his name to Sun Myung Moon when he became an itinerant preacher.

At the time of the Reverend Moon's birth, my country was suffering under the yoke of Japanese occupation. Japan had colonized Korea in 1905, an occupation that did not end until after World War II. Christians then composed less than 1 percent of the Korean population, but Christianity developed an ardent following in our stratified society. Protestant missionaries had arrived in Korea from Europe in the mid-1880s. They had survived despite their opposition to ancestor worship, in part because Christianity taught that everyone was a child of

God, something of a revolutionary idea in what was still a rigid, feudal society.

Even the aristocracy in the ancient Korean kingdom of Silla was classified according to what was known as the bone-rank system, or *kolp'un-je.* The elite were divided into three classes: the *songgol,* or holy bone class, from which the sacred kings sprang; the *chin'gol,* the true bone class or the upper aristocracy; and the *tup'um,* head classes, which included all other members of the aristocracy. This would influence Sun Myung Moon's organization of his own religion.

Most Koreans, of course, were poor farmers, not aristocrats. Christianity offered them the hope that if there was no equality on earth, there would be in Heaven. Though small in number, the Christian churches became a center of resistance to the occupying forces. A year before Sun Myung Moon was born, a declaration of independence from colonial Japan was drafted, on March 1, 1919, by a coalition of Protestant ministers, Buddhist monks, and leaders of the many messianic religious sects then gaining popularity in Korea. The signatories were arrested and jailed.

Despite that setback, many Christian leaders — those who did not collaborate — stepped up their agitation for an end to Japanese occupation after the colonial government imposed Japanese as the national language of Korea and established the Shinto shrine in 1925. Korean schoolchildren were required to acknowledge the divinity of the Japanese emperor and to attend sacred rites for his ancestors. Every Korean family was ordered to erect a Shinto shrine in its home. Two thousand Christians who refused were imprisoned; dozens were executed.

By the time the Reverend Moon's family converted to Presbyterianism, in 1930, the economic hardship of Japanese occupation was as evident as the religious persecution. Nearly all

Korean farmers were tenants. Although they were producing record amounts of rice, most of it was exported to Japan, while the local populace went hungry. Japanese nationals made up only 5 percent of the workforce but they held most of the top industrial jobs. Japanese firms owned 92 percent of the working mines in 1932, for example, but it was Korean miners who toiled below ground and lived in unheated shacks above. Those Koreans fortunate enough to secure positions with the government were restricted to low-level jobs.

Such oppression was the backdrop to Sun Myung Moon's childhood. He is said to have been a studious and prayerful boy, a devout Presbyterian following his family's conversion when he was ten. All that changed on Easter morning in 1936, when Sun Myung Moon was sixteen. He had been deep in prayer on a mountainside when, he says, Jesus appeared to him and told him that God wanted him to complete the work Jesus himself had left unfinished on earth. While Jesus' death on the cross had delivered spiritual salvation to mankind, his crucifixion came before he could complete his mission to bring physical salvation to man by restoring the Garden of Eden on earth.

At first the boy refused to listen, but Jesus persuaded Sun Myung Moon that Korea was the new Israel, the land chosen by God for the Second Coming. It was up to him to establish the True Family of God on earth. The Reverend Moon would later write about this vision: "Early in my life God called me for a mission as His instrument. . . . I committed myself unyieldingly in pursuit of truth, searching the hills and valleys of the spiritual world. The time suddenly came to me when heaven opened up, and I was privileged to communicate with Jesus Christ and the living God directly. Since then I have received many astonishing revelations."

Sun Myung Moon never had any formal theological training. Two years after his original vision, he went to Seoul to
learn electrical engineering and from there to Japan to continue those studies at Waseda University in 1941. There,
according to church historians, he joined an underground
movement to work to end the occupation of Korea. He continued his personal search for truth by traveling into the spirit
world himself to speak directly to Jesus, to Moses, to Buddha,
to Satan, and to God himself. How he accomplished this trans-
figuration is one of Unificationism's mysteries.

The Reverend Moon's teachings are contained in *Divine
Principle*, a document shaped over many years by the revelations the Reverend Moon says he received through prayer,
study of the Bible, and his own conversations with God and
the great prophets. *Divine Principle* is the central text of the
Unification Church, but it was not actually written by Sun
Myung Moon. Hyo Won Eu, the first president of the church
and one of the Reverend Moon's earliest disciples, wrote *Divine
Principle* based on the Reverend Moon's notes and their conversations about his revelations.

Kwang Yol Yoo, a Unificationist biographer, writes that the
Reverend Moon could not transcribe his divine revelations fast
enough. "He wrote very fast with a pencil in his notebook.
One person beside him would sharpen his pencil, and he
couldn't follow his writing speed. By the time Father's pencil
got thick, this next person could not sharpen another pencil,
he wrote so very fast. That was the beginning of the Divine
Principle book."

For a heavenly inspired document, *Divine Principle* is
awfully derivative. The 556-page sacred text of the Unification Church is a synthesis of Shamanism, Buddhism, neo-
Confucianism, and Christianity. It borrows from the Bible, from

Eastern philosophy, from Korean legend, and from the popular religious movements of the Reverend Moon's youth to stitch together a patchwork theology, with the Reverend Moon at its center.

The modern roots of the Unification Church can be found in Ch'ondogyo — the religion of the Heavenly Way — originally called Tonghak, or Eastern Learning, a nineteenth-century sect closely tied to Korean traditional religion. Like the Unification Church, Ch'ondogyo taught that every individual's spirit is created by God, that our souls are everlasting, and that all religions one day will be unified.

Even the Unification Church's central tenet, that the Fall was caused not by Eve's eating a forbidden fruit but by Eve's having sexual intercourse with Satan, is not an idea that originated with the Reverend Moon. He was taught that theory in 1945 when he studied for six months with a visionary named Baek Moon Kim at the Israel Monastery in Seoul. Kim taught that the Garden of Eden could be restored only through blood purification. Eve's sin, the theory holds, has been transmitted to new generations through Satan's bloodlines. It was part of Jesus' mission to purify man's bloodlines by marrying and producing sinless children. He was killed before he could do what God intended. As a result, Jesus' death brought spiritual but not physical salvation to the world.

Kim was not alone in this belief. Kim Seongdo was the founder of the Holy Lord Church in 1935 in Chulson in North Korea. She claimed that Jesus had appeared to her and given her a similar explanation about the sexual nature of the Fall and promised that the new Messiah would return to Korea. She taught her followers that sexual abstinence, even in marriage, was necessary to create an environment pure enough to receive the Lord of the Second Advent. After her death, her followers joined the Unification Church and accepted the Reverend Moon as the Messiah.

Divine Principle acknowledges its debt to the long messianic tradition in Korean religious thought.

> The Korean nation, as the Third Israel, has believed since the 500-year reign of the Yi Dynasty the prophecy that the King of Righteousness would appear in that land, and, establishing the Millennium, would come to receive tributes from all the countries of the world. This faith has encouraged the people to undergo the bitter course of history, waiting for the time to come. This was truly the Messianic idea of the Korean people which they believed according to *Chung Gam Nok,* a book of prophecy. . . . Interpreted correctly, the King of Righteousness, Chung-Do Ryung (the person coming with God's word), is a Korean-style name for the Lord of the Second Advent. God revealed through Chung Gam Nok, before the introduction of Christianity in Korea, that the Messiah would come again, at a later time, in Korea. Today, many scholars have come to ascertain that most of the prophecies written in this book coincide with those in the Bible.

The Unification Church teaches that God chose Sun Myung Moon to fulfill that role. The introduction to *Divine Principle,* published by the Unification Church in 1973, is explicit on this point. "With the fullness of time, God has sent His messenger to resolve the fundamental questions of life and the universe. His name is Sun Myung Moon. For many decades he wandered in a vast spiritual world in search of the ultimate truth. On this path, he endured suffering unimagined by anyone in human history. God alone will remember it. Knowing that no one can find the ultimate truth to save mankind without going through the bitterest of trials, he fought alone against myriads of satanic forces, both in the spiritual and physical worlds, and finally triumphed over them all."

The Reverend Moon's task was to fulfill the mission of Jesus. He would marry a perfect woman and restore mankind to the state of perfection that existed in the Garden of Eden. He and his wife would be the world's True Parents. They would be sinless, as would their children. Couples blessed by the Reverend Moon would become part of his pure-blood lineage and be assured a place in Heaven.

As individuals, we all have an active role to play in this restoration drama. Before the Messiah can fully establish Heaven on earth, mankind must make amends for the sins of the past. In Unificationist terms, they must pay "indemnity" to compensate God for humanity's past failures. The Unification Church's strict rules of behavior — no smoking, no drinking, no gambling, no sex outside of marriage — are designed to help individuals in that task.

"The conclusion of the Principle is that you must make up your own mind to love True Parents more than your own self, spouse or children," Sun Myung Moon has written. "Ultimately, the True Father is the axis around which all children and posterity are centered."

The Reverend Moon's own life is said to be a model of willing sacrifice and patient suffering. According to church historians, he was first arrested in 1945 on a charge of using counterfeit money to buy apples by Communist officials who suspected he was a spy from the south.

When he began his public ministry in Pyongyang, his ideas were rejected as heresy by Christian ministers and denounced by local Communist authorities. It was 1947. The city was occupied by Soviet troops. Korea would soon be formally divided into two states, the Communist North under Soviet domination and the democratic South under the influence of the United States. The Communist authorities are said to have tortured Sun Myung Moon and tossed his body outside the prison gates, where he was retrieved and nursed back to health by one of his early disciples, Won Pil Kim. The Reverend Moon resumed preaching despite the ban on religious teaching by Communist authorities.

He was not to be free for long. The Reverend Moon was arrested again in 1948, this time for "advocating chaos in society." He was convicted and sent to Hungnam prison, a hard-labor camp where prisoners often were worked to death. By his own account, as prisoner no. 596, the Reverend Moon was underfed and overworked, filling hundred-pound bags with fertilizer and loading them onto railroad cars. The ammonium sulfate in the fertilizer burned the skin on his hands, but he never complained during his two years and eight months in the camp.

"I never prayed from weakness. I never asked for help. How could I tell God, my Father, about my suffering and cause his heart to grieve still more. I could only tell him I would never be defeated by my suffering," he wrote.

The roots of the Unification Church's adamant opposition to international Communism are grounded in the Reverend Moon's personal experiences. His anti-Communist political beliefs would become a fundamental tenet of his religious philosophy. Those convictions would align him with the anti-Communist governments of South Korea, no matter how oppressive, for the rest of the century.

While he was imprisoned, North Korea invaded the south, provoking the civil war that led to the formal political division of the peninsula. United Nations forces pushed Communist troops north of the thirty-eighth parallel, and in October of 1950, UN troops liberated Hungnam prison, one day before Moon claims he was scheduled to be executed. When he was freed, the Reverend Moon and two disciples, Won Pil Kim and Chung Hwa Pak, began the long journey to South Korea on foot. According to church legend, the Reverend Moon carried Pak on his back for hundreds of miles after Pak injured a leg. A grainy photograph of this feat is something of an icon in the Unification Church.

The Reverend Moon settled in the port city of Pusan in 1951, building his first church by hand on a small hillside. With a dirt floor, mud walls, and a roof constructed from wood scraps and army ration boxes, the church was little more than a mud hut. The city was crowded with soldiers and refugees displaced by the war. The Reverend Moon worked by day as a dock laborer and resumed his preaching at night.

The Reverend Moon's official biographers skip over the fact that Sun Myung Moon had married in April 1945 at age twenty-five. His wife, Sungil Choi, gave birth to a son, Sung Jin, one year later. They were living in Seoul on June 6, 1946, when the Reverend Moon went to the marketplace to buy rice. En route, he now says, God appeared to him and instructed him to leave immediately for northern Korea to preach. Sun Myung Moon, who teaches that he is the ideal Father of all God's children, abandoned his wife and three-month-old son without explanation. They did not see or hear from him again for six years.

It was not until the Reverend Moon arrived in Pusan with his disciples in 1951 that Sungil Choi was reunited with her husband. They did not stay together long. His wife and son moved with the Reverend Moon to Seoul in 1954, where he founded the Unification Church, known formally as the Holy

Spirit Association for the Unification of World Christianity, but the marriage soon broke up. The Reverend Moon dismisses this marriage in a single sentence: "With the Christian people opposing our movement, my first wife was influenced and, being weak, that caused the rupture in my family and I got divorced," he has written. It was as though Sungil Choi and their son, Sung Jin, ceased to exist.

"Rev. Moon's wife became increasingly unhappy with Rev. Moon's dedication to the members who joined his movement, and finally demanded a divorce," Hendrik Dijk wrote in an internal history of the church. "Rev. Moon did not want this, but finally the situation became irresolvable, and he granted her the divorce. She was in the position to follow him, but found herself unable to do so. She also differed with him theologically and thought the Messiah would return on the clouds. She was strongly influenced by the negativity of the Christian churches."

His wife's departure coincided with the first published reports of sexual abuse in the Unification Church. Rumors were rife that the Reverend Moon required female acolytes to have sex with him as a religious initiation rite. Some religious sects at the time did practice ritual nudity and reportedly forced members to have sexual intercourse with a messianic leader in a purification rite known as *p'i kareun*. The Reverend Moon has always denied these reports, claiming they were part of efforts by mainstream religious leaders to discredit the Unification Church.

In the early days of the Unification Church, members met in a small house with two rooms. It was known as the House of Three Doors. It was rumored that at the first door one was made to take off one's jacket, at the second door one's outer clothing, and at the third one's undergarments in preparation for sex. There was an apocryphal story of the woman who went to church wearing no fewer than seven layers of clothing, hoping to thwart any attempt to undress her.

With these stories in wide circulation in July 1955, the Reverend Moon was arrested for gross immorality and draft evasion. Both charges were eventually dropped, but rumors persisted that the church practiced *p'i kareun*.

Mrs. Gil Ja Sa Eu, the wife of the first president of the Unification Church — the man who wrote the *Divine Principle* — was one of five professors and fourteen students expelled from Ewha University in Seoul because administrators there believed the rumors about the Unification Church.

In a speech in 1987, Mrs. Eu traced the origin of those stories back to the Holy Lord Church of Kim Seongdo. Because they prayed so devoutly, Mrs. Eu said, "many people in that group received that they were being restored to the position of Adam and Eve before the Fall. Therefore, they felt totally purified, with no sin. They said, 'We are like Adam and Eve, who were naked and unashamed!' So one time, out of great joy, they took off their clothes and danced naked. This event spread all over Korea and, despite its very remote relationship to the Unification Church, it became one cause for the persecution of our church from other Christians."

The record of those early days became all the more confused in 1993 when Chung Hwa Pak, the disciple whom the Reverend Moon is reputed to have carried on his back to South Korea in 1951, published a book entitled *The Tragedy of the Six Marias*. In it Pak states that the Reverend Moon did practice *p'i kareun* and contends that the Reverend Moon's first wife left him because of his sexual activities with other women. The Reverend Moon is said by Pak to have impregnated a university student, Myung Hee Kim, in 1953 while he was still married. Because adultery was a criminal offense in Korea, the

Reverend Moon sent his lover to Japan to give birth. A son, Hee Jin, was born in 1954 and was acknowledged to be the son of the Reverend Moon. The boy would die in a train accident thirteen years later.

Chung Hwa Pak was persuaded by the Reverend Moon to rejoin the church after publishing his memoir. He disavowed his account of the early days of the Unification Church. I've always wondered what the price was of that retraction.

My own parents saw no evidence of sexual misconduct when they were each recruited independently to join the church in Seoul. By 1957 the Unification Church had a presence in thirty Korean cities and towns. Though they came from different places and disparate backgrounds, my parents were attracted to the Unification Church out of the same sense of idealism. Religion had not been central to the life of either of them as children. They were like so many young Koreans in the late 1950s, reeling from civil war and searching for a way to help their divided, destitute land. My mother and father, each in their own way, were looking for a purpose in life larger than themselves.

My father, Sung Pyo Hong, joined the church in 1957. He had been sent to the city by his parents, to study pharmacy, from the small town of Ok-Gya, South Cholla province, where his family grew rice and barley on a small farm. That farm, according to tradition, would be inherited by his older brother. He and his three sisters would make other lives for themselves.

He liked the city. He was a good student and a grateful son, so he was torn when his parents expressed their disapproval when he told them of his interest in a new religious sect. He had been recruited into the Unification Church, as most new members are, on the street. He and a friend were invited to attend a lecture by one of the Reverend Moon's early disciples. My father came away intrigued.

Soon he was attending lectures regularly and acting as care-taker for the church. During summers and school holidays, he went out preaching, trying to recruit new members. He worked tirelessly for the Reverend Moon, but he did not give up his studies, as so many recruits do.

My mother, Gil Ja Yoo, had grown up in Gil-Ju in what is now North Korea. Her family was part of the mass exodus of refugees who came to South Korea in the 1940s. She was study-ing for her college entrance examinations when she, too, was invited to attend a lecture at the Unification Church. A religious life was not what she had planned. My mother was a talented classical pianist and dreamed of a career on the concert stage.

Her parents were even more adamant in their opposition to the Reverend Moon and his church than my father's family. My grandmother was especially fierce in her disapproval. She for-bade my mother to go to church. My mother, nonetheless, would sneak out of the house to attend services. More than once, she was caught and beaten by one of her brothers as punishment for her defiance.

Most Koreans were like my grandparents; they considered the Unification Church a bizarre, if not dangerous, cult. In 1960 their concerns were heightened when the Reverend Moon selected the bride who would serve as True Mother to the family of man. Hak Ja Han was only seventeen years old when the forty-year-old Reverend Moon chose her to be his wife. Her mother had been a devout follower of Kim Seongdo and believed the Reverend Moon to be the Lord of the Second Advent. She was happy to give her daughter for God, to become the True Mother of the True Family.

"The fall of man can be condensed into one sentence: human beings lost their parents," Sun Myung Moon has writ-ten of Adam and Eve's being cast out of the Garden of Eden.

"The history of man has been a search for parents. The day people meet their True Parents is their greatest day because, until then, everyone is like an orphan living in an orphanage. You have no place to call true home."

The Reverend Moon never spoke to me about his own father, but he spoke with great respect for his mother and her capacity for hard work. His cousin remembers True Father as the smart, favored child of six daughters and two sons. Two other babies, a set of twins, had died in infancy. Young Ki Moon, one of the Reverend Moon's cousins, spoke at a memorial service in Korea in 1989 commemorating the birth of Kyung Kye Kim, the Reverend Moon's mother. His cousin recalled the Reverend Moon as "very mischievous when he was a boy. One day when he was six years old big mother spanked him so much that he nearly fainted. I think after this incident big mother was shocked and I never heard her scolding him again."

It was his mother who recognized Sun Myung Moon's intellectual gifts, according to his cousin. She was desperate for him to have a university education. "He had to go to Japan for further study but there was no money to send him, so he had to return to his hometown," his cousin recalled. "Big mother wanted to sell the land that was in my father's name to pay True Father's tuition in Japan. Since all the land was in my father's name, she couldn't sell it. So she told me to borrow my mother's stamp so that she could sell the land and send True Father to school in Japan." This deceit was part of God's plan for the Messiah. In order to support the divine plan for the Messiah, others in the Moon family had to suffer.

Hak Ja Han's childhood had centered on the spiritual movements with which her mother identified. She led a sheltered, protected life on Jejudo Island until 1955, when she and her mother moved to Seoul. She was reared by her grandmother, her mother being so engrossed in her own religious life. Her father had abandoned the family when she was still small. When Hak Ja Han was eleven years old, her mother became cook to Sun Myung Moon. Hak Ja Han was still a child when the Messiah first met her and made his decision to marry her.

As the Reverend Moon later recalled,

> *Women of the early Unification Church wanted to love me at the risk of their lives, coming to see me even late at night. So people gossiped about us. The women didn't even know why they made such visits to a man who they knew remained centered on God. And when the Holy Wedding came, even the elderly widows wanted to be able to stand in the position of Mother. Some women even claimed to be the True Mother, their eyes shining with confidence. An old lady of 70 years said she would become my wife and bear 10 children! Of course, she didn't know why she was saying such things. Women with daughters prayed to God with deep sincerity and said they received revelations that their daughters would become the True Mother.*
>
> *But the woman who would become the True Mother appeared unexpectedly. She was a person whom few had met. . . . I was 40 and about to marry a 17-year-old girl. If this were not God's will, who could be crazier than I? Just imagine, from that time on Mother's great responsibility was to carry all the burdens of the Unification Church. Many wonderful, college-educated women were lining up and listing their qualifications, but I shook them all off and chose an innocent 17-year-old girl as Mother. What a surprise it was! Old ladies and mothers exclaimed and rolled their eyes!*

Youth should not be a barrier to marriage, the Reverend Moon told his followers: "As soon as you notice your child is an adolescent and aware of sex, they are blessed in marriage. Why should they fall? God, or Heaven, is responsible to each person on Earth to feed, to educate, and to marry. Nowadays, people work hard and yet do not have enough food. People are ready to marry but they cannot. . . . Why should someone be left after one has started to have the impulse of love? It is the parents' responsibility to determine the proper time."

Sun Myung Moon and Hak Ja Han were married on April 11, 1960, at the church's headquarters in Seoul. A dozen members had recently left the church, carrying stories about the Reverend Moon's claim to be the Messiah and his practice of personally choosing marriage partners for his disciples. There were protests from the outraged parents of church members on the street outside as Sun Myung Moon and Hak Ja Han were joined in holy matrimony.

The opposition was as providential as the wedding, in the Reverend Moon's view. "Jesus was persecuted by the nation, by the priests, by everyone. Unless we are in the same situation as Jesus was, the restoration cannot be done. This is why the entire Korean nation was mobilized to persecute us. We held the Wedding while hearing voices opposing us from outside the gates. By doing this, the Unification Church gained the victory in the midst of battle. If we had not done so, God would not have rejoiced."

A week later, the Reverend Moon joined his three closest disciples — Won Pil Kim, Hyo Won Eu, and Young Whi Kim — in marriage to church women he had selected as brides for them. These weddings were followed within a year by thirty-three more arranged marriages, my parents' among them. The Reverend Moon had given my father the option of selecting his own bride, an unusual opportunity because the church teaches that marriage is a spiritual union that should not be influenced by such distractions as physical attraction. My father deferred to the Reverend Moon's judgment.

My parents did not know one another when the Reverend Moon made the match, but both were trusting when he said that he had paired them because he knew they would have children who would bring credit to them and to the Unification Church.

When my grandmother got wind of the pending nuptials, she hid my mother's shoes and locked her in her room. My mother appealed to her younger brother to help her. He found her shoes and unlocked the door. She ran all the way to church. My grandmother was not far behind. She was, however, too late. By the time my parents heard her shouting and banging on the doors of the church, the Reverend Moon had already blessed their marriage.

The Reverend Moon has never forgotten how my grandmother burst into the church that day, beating on his chest with her fists, denouncing him for marrying off her daughter to a man she did not know, in a church she did not trust. Over time, Sun Myung Moon and I both came to believe that I had inherited my grandmother's spirit.

2

My earliest memory is of a small, dark room at the end of a long, narrow hallway. If there are windows, I can't see them in my mind's eye. If there are furnishings, I can't envision them. I see only a tiny version of myself, seated on the bare floor, encircled by darkness.

I am alone. The house is empty, but, curiously, I am not afraid. What I am feeling is closer to resignation, an odd emotion to associate with a little girl not much bigger than a toddler. But that's what I felt even then, that my place in the world was fated and that my role in life was to endure.

I don't know who I am waiting for — my brother to come home from school, a baby-sitter to come from church — but I do know who I do not expect to see coming down that long, narrow hallway. My mother was away for most of my childhood. I spent my earliest years missing her with a longing that was deep and unarticulated, a physical ache in the hollow center of my heart. Like my father, she was filled with the passion of a freshly minted religious convert. As the first disciples of the Reverend Sun Myung Moon, my parents saw it as their mission to spread the word that the Lord of the Second Advent had come and to recruit new, even more impassioned members for the fledgling Unification Church.

Children complicated that mission, even as our very existence was an expression of it. The Reverend Moon instructed the original thirty-six Blessed Couples to have as many children as possible in order to build the foundation of the True Family of God. He expected them simultaneously to travel throughout Korea, and eventually the world, preaching and "witnessing" on his behalf. The Reverend Moon taught his followers that God would take care of their children if his followers took care of him. The urgency of the Reverend Moon's mission superseded the personal bond between mother and child.

It was my parents' religious duty to bring us into the world, but from an early age I knew that their first responsibility was to the Reverend Moon, not to us. They fed us. They clothed us. They sheltered us. I know that they loved us. But the one thing that children most crave — their parents' time and attention — ours could not give to us.

I was the second of seven children born to Gil Ja Yoo and Sung Pyo Hong within the first twelve years of their marriage. I was born on a bedroll on the floor of our maternal grandmother's small house in Seoul. My grandmother had never forgiven her daughter for joining what she and most Koreans thought to be a crazy religious cult, but she never turned my mother away.

The church itself had no money to share, so the Reverend Moon sent his disciples across the country fortified with little more than their own fervor to survive. My parents did not travel together. To maximize their impact, the Reverend Moon ordered his disciples to spread out, to witness alone. My mother and father would set off in separate directions to Korea's small towns and even smaller villages.

We would be left to the care of our grandmother, an assortment of aunts, or the women we called the sisters, unmarried church members who served the Reverend Moon by babysitting the children of married disciples. Once I had my own children, it was even more difficult for me to understand how my parents could have done this, could have abandoned their babies so completely to the care of others, often strangers. How was this a model of a perfect family?

I do know that my brothers and sisters and I were luckier than some children. Some of the Reverend Moon's followers simply left their sons and daughters in orphanages in order to preach the word. A few never returned for them.

In 1965 the Reverend Moon described his ideal circumstances for the rearing of children: "We would like to see a boarding house for the children of our members, where some responsible persons could raise them and educate them at least for a few years. This would release you for your necessary witnessing. We have people in our group who are well qualified and willing to conduct such a boarding house and school. This is in the future when we have more money to support such a house and the children. It will be very good for the children, good for the parents, and very good for the movement. No one can enter the Kingdom of Heaven as an individual, but as a family." He urged his early disciples, my parents among them, to "find people who have the wealth to help us finance such a school."

Hard as it was for me to be separated from my mother, life was no easier for her. Travel was difficult. She would beg or borrow money for a train ticket, hitch a ride on a hay wagon, do whatever it took to bring the message of the new Messiah into the countryside. Her reward was often the hostility of her audience. Early members of the Unification Church were mocked and stoned, spit upon and jeered. Only occasionally were they heard.

My mother combatted the constant assault on her spirit with fervent prayer. While prayer replenished her soul, it did little for her belly, which was often swollen both with hunger and with child. She lived on rice and water, on the charity of farm women who would see her pregnant profile and take pity on her. I think of the ravenous appetite that marked my own pregnancies and I am amazed at the deprivation my mother suffered in silence.

Her days were long and repetitive. She would rent a room in a village house and spend her days preaching on street corners, her nights lecturing in nearly empty community halls. She had been shy as a girl, but she turned herself during those years into a powerful speaker. She never learned to enjoy the spotlight, but over time she conquered her fear and began to command attention when she spoke.

Poverty and separation were not my parents' only hardship in the early years of their marriage. When I was still nursing at my mother's breast, soldiers burst into the small room my family rented in Seoul. The soldiers ordered my father out of the house and, while my mother looked on in terror, marched him off to prison. My father's crime was failing to register with the army. In Korea military service was compulsory for young men. He had not deliberately evaded his military duty, he told me later. He had been assured that an exemption had been arranged.

The soldiers did not tell my mother where they were taking my father that day. With me in her arms and my two-year-old brother, Jin, in tow, she walked from jail to jail, from police station to station all across Seoul until she found him. It never occurred to my mother to go directly to the Reverend Moon for help. He was too important a figure to bother with her personal problems, no matter how pressing. During my father's absence, she struggled mightily to keep the three of us housed and fed.

Throughout it all, my parents never complained. They were doing the work of God. They considered their poverty ennobling. They accepted their tribulations as infinitesimal compared with the suffering that the Reverend Moon had endured in the formative years of the Unification Church: his imprisonments, his persecution at the hands of the godless Communists, his long march south. The story of Sun Myung Moon's trials already had taken on the proportion of legend. By then, however, the Reverend Moon was living very well indeed, especially in contrast with his disciples.

The Moon family occupied spacious rooms above the church headquarters, which were located in one of Seoul's better neighborhoods. They were supported by the labor of the Reverend Moon's followers, who served him and his family at table, cared for his children, cleaned their house, and washed their clothes.

For most of my early childhood, we lived in a series of single rooms that we rented in houses in a Seoul slum known as Moontown. The name had nothing to do with the Reverend Moon or the Unification Church. The neighborhood was located on a treeless hillside high above the South Korean capital and, hence, closer to the moon. It was a ghetto of small, dilapidated houses packed closely together on narrow, winding streets. The houses were all the same — single-story structures heated by coal stoves. Every house was topped with a tiled roof and surrounded by a gated stone wall, the top of which was embedded with shards of broken glass to discourage the thieves who roamed the area.

We lived in so many different rooms in Moontown that they blend together in my memory. I remember the outdoor steps of one house, where Jin and I played "family," feeding our baby sister, Choong Sook, pebbles that she obediently licked until a church sister stopped us. I remember another house where we rented two rooms at opposite ends of a long corridor. A sister lived in one room with us children; my parents had a small room of their own. One day the couple who owned the house accused my parents of stealing coal. The sister became so upset at this assault on my parents' honesty that she protested angrily to our landlords, who promptly tossed all of us into the street.

The room I remember best was the scene of my warmest memory of my father. It was a large room divided by a small chest of drawers. My mother had just given birth to her fifth child, my sister Chang Sook. One of my aunts had come to help out. We four older children slept with my aunt on bedrolls on one side of the chest; my parents slept with the new baby on a futon on the other.

Ours was the darker side of the room. I longed to sleep closer to my parents, closer to the light. As evening fell one night, I pretended to fall asleep on my parents' side of the chest. I prayed they would let me stay, snuggled next to them for the night.

It was not to be. My father picked me up and carried me back to the dark side of the room. It was the most physical contact I remember having with him. I can still feel the ease with which he lifted me from the floor, the soft brush of his shirt against my cheek. I was so happy, having him hold me, that it took the sting out of my sadness at having to sleep so far away from him and my mother, so far away from the light.

That moment of intimacy is so vivid, I think, because such moments were so rare. Ours was a life of numbing routine and grinding poverty. What intimacy there was was the forced communal intimacy of the poor. There was no indoor plumbing in Moontown. We washed our faces and brushed our teeth at a public tap in an alley behind the house. We relieved ourselves in the festering latrines that served the entire neighborhood.

Trucks would patrol Moontown to drain the latrines but they never came often enough. I would delay a trip out back as long as I could. When I could wait no longer, I would hold my breath when I pushed open the door to the outhouse. The stench of human waste was overwhelming, even in the freezing months of winter. In the summer the flies were everywhere. If I took my fingers from my nose long enough to shoo them away, I would have to gag back the vomit in my throat. I would burst out of the latrine gasping for air.

Once a week my entire family would march down to the public bathhouse for a proper scrubbing. Each of us carried a small metal bucket, with our cake of soap, our shampoo, a towel, and a clean change of clothes. We would pay our coins and the boys would enter through one door, the girls through another. Inside were two large rooms, each equipped with enormous, steaming hot pools. I can still see the dozens of women and girls sitting side by side, our naked skin turning pink in the hot water. There were ladies employed by the bathhouse who would scrub the backs of our wealthier neighbors for a small fee. We would rinse off in the public showers and head home physically cleansed for another week.

We were children, and children have no sense of the economic scale of things. We did not think ourselves especially poor or deprived. We were, after all, no different from our neighbors to the left and to the right. We played paper dolls on the steps and jacks on the broken sidewalks. We chased each other through the congested streets on our way to even more

congested classrooms. We fought and laughed in the same proportion as those better off than we.

What set us apart was not money but faith. From the start I
knew that our religion made our family different, that being a
member of the Unification Church was not like being a Presbyterian or a Buddhist. I did not talk about my faith except with
my friends at church. I knew that others thought our beliefs
odd, even dangerous. I was content not to call attention to my
religion, but I was neither especially ashamed nor particularly
proud of it as a young child. Except perhaps at Christmas. At
Christmas I longed for our family to be like the families of my
nonchurch friends.

Christmas trees and elaborate celebrations of the birth of
Jesus were rare in Moontown because of the impoverishment
that defined the neighborhood. But Santa Claus comes even to
the poor in Seoul. He never came to our rented rooms. Every
year I would go to sleep on Christmas Eve, secretly believing
that this would be the year that Santa Claus would leave a
small toy at the head of my bedroll, just as he did for all my
friends. Every Christmas morning, I would choke back salty
tears when I realized that, once again, he had not remembered
me or my brothers and sisters.

It was not cruelty on my parents' part. They were so busy
working to establish the church, their minds and hearts were
so focused on their mission for the Reverend Moon that, my
mother now tells me, it never even crossed her mind to buy us
Christmas gifts. We observed Christmas as a day to commit
ourselves to the teachings of Jesus. Even though we were
taught that Jesus had failed to complete the mission God
intended for him, we were encouraged to acknowledge his
many spiritual accomplishments by marking the day of his
birth. The best way for adults to do that, according to the Rev-

erend Moon, was to spend the day recruiting for the Unification Church.

We could not make Santa Claus come to our rooms, but we took our pleasure where we found it. My brother Jin used to walk the streets of Moontown searching the windows for the telltale blue glow that signaled the rare house with a television set. He would hope for an unlocked door and, on finding it so, tiptoe into the room where a family would be gathered around the TV. He would sometimes be able to watch an entire program before someone detected the stranger in their midst and chased him back into the street.

I was as admiring as I was shocked by my brother's boldness. I could not imagine being so forward. Maybe because of all the time I spent alone when I was small, I was uncomfortable with people, even with my relatives. For a year, when I was four years old and Jin was six, we were sent two hundred miles away to live with my mother's sister and her husband in Korea's second-largest city, Pusan. Our parents simply could not afford to feed and house their growing family. Our aunt and uncle were childless. They ran a small pharmacy and lived in a single room upstairs.

They were kind to us, but both Jin and I longed for home. There was a back room to the store, where I stayed and played alone while my aunt and uncle worked. I can still remember my happiness when Jin would join me there after he returned from school. We would sneak little treats, especially a health drink called Pakhasu, out of the store and into the back room to enjoy clandestinely, an act of subterfuge I would never have dared on my own.

My little sister Choong Sook had been sent at the same time to live with my maternal grandparents in their two-bedroom house in Seoul. My mother's older brother was living there with his wife, too. They had no children themselves, and my aunt adored my little sister, treating her more like a daughter than a niece.

My mother later confessed that she regretted sending us all away for so long, that she wished she had found a way to keep her family together while she served the Reverend Moon. At the time, though, he was her priority, not us. It was not the last, or even the deepest, regret my parents would have about the sacrifices they expected their children to make in the name of Sun Myung Moon and his church.

As soon as I returned from Pusan, my mother enrolled me in public school. I was only five, a full year younger than all of my classmates. After so much time alone, the sight of this noisy schoolhouse overflowing with rambunctious children filled me with terror. On as many mornings as not, I would refuse to go in. This strategy backfired, of course. A teacher would have to come and get me, calling all the more unwanted attention to me as I was dragged into the classroom.

There were as many as eighty children packed into every classroom of my elementary school. I was miserable, lost in the crowd, too shy to communicate even my most basic needs. I can still recall the cruel laughter of my classmates as a puddle of urine formed beneath my desk. I had been too scared to tell the teacher I needed to use the bathroom.

I was more at home in the church, which was central to our lives from the very beginning. In place of fairy tales at bedtime, our mother told us inspirational stories about the life of the Reverend Moon. We knew his biography better than we knew our own. Hanging photographs of the Reverend Moon and the True Family was one of our first rituals each time we rented a new room. That room would also have a shrine. In the center would be a picture of True Parents, surrounded by flowers and *shimjung,* or heart, candles. The candles were blessed by the Reverend Moon and believed to weaken Satan's power.

Sunday is the day of worship in the Unification Church, although our day begins much earlier and lasts much longer than that of mainstream Christian sects. We rise before dawn to prepare for the Pledge Service, which begins at 5:00 A.M. Even the youngest children and babes in arms are expected to attend. Oh, how we hated to rise so early when we were small! The Pledge is also recited on the first day of each month and on church holidays.

Once we stumbled from our sleep, we would gather before the shrine. We would bow three times — to represent a bow to God, True Father, and True Mother — and then we would recite the words entitled "My Pledge." I had memorized every word by the time I was seven years old.

1. As the center of the cosmos, I will fulfill our Father's will [purpose of creation], and the responsibility given to me [for self-perfection]. I will become a dutiful daughter and a child of goodness to attend our Father forever in the ideal world of creation by returning joy and glory to Him. This I pledge.

2. I will take upon myself completely the will of God to give me the whole creation as my inheritance. He has given me His word, His personality, and His Heart, and is reviving me who had died, making me one with Him and His true child. To do this, our Father has persevered for 6,000 years the sacrificial way of the cross. This I pledge.

3. As a true daughter, I will follow our Father's pattern and charge bravely forward into the enemy camp, until I have judged them completely with the weapons with which He has been defeating the enemy Satan for me throughout the course of history, by sowing sweat for earth, tears for man, and blood for heaven, as a servant but with a Father's heart, in order to restore His children and the universe lost to Satan. This I pledge.

4. The individual, family, society, nation, world, and cosmos who are willing to attend our Father, the source of peace, happiness, freedom, and all ideals, will fulfill the ideal world of one heart in one body by restoring their original nature. To do this, I will become a true daughter, returning joy and satisfaction to our Father, and as our Father's representative, I will transfer to the creation peace, happiness, freedom, and all ideals in the world of the heart. This I pledge.

5. I am proud of the one Sovereignty, proud of the one people, proud of the one land, proud of the one language and culture centered upon God, proud of becoming the child of the One True Parent, proud of the family who is to inherit one tradition, proud of being a laborer who is working to establish the one world of the heart.

I will fight with my life.
I will be responsible for accomplishing my duty and mission.
This I pledge and swear.
This I pledge and swear.
This I pledge and swear.

After the Pledge Service, our parents would leave us to go to hear the Reverend Moon preach at church headquarters at 6:00 A.M. He would sometimes talk for hours; as many as fifteen hours was not unusual. He would be annoyed if anyone in the congregation left to use the bathroom during his sermons, so Sundays could be quite an ordeal for adults seated on the wooden floor of the church's main meeting hall.

I began to attend Sunday school as a very small child. It was a long trip from Moontown, requiring several bus changes. My mother would slip our bus fare and offering coins into one of Jin's hands and my own hand into his other. I wore a red cotton knitted hat that tied under my chin. In my memory, I am always looking up at my brother's kind face as we walk hand in hand down the street.

I always looked up to Jin. Even as a boy, he had a wisdom beyond his years. He was kind in a way that I knew I was not. When we played school, he would be the teacher and my little sister and I the students. When Choong Sook did not know the answer to a question, he would help her. I am ashamed to remember how I would scream and yell that he was being unfair, that she was cheating, that he was giving her an undue advantage. How patient he was as he explained the need for older ones to help teach the younger ones! I was secretly humiliated by his goodness, but I was a stubborn girl. I could never admit that I was wrong. Invariably, it would be Jin who would apologize after an argument that I myself had provoked.

My brother was no saint, though. Jin had a mischievous side. There was a market near one of the bus stops on the way to church. Jin and I would sometimes go there, instead of Sunday school, spending my mother's coins on treats. We did not eat well at home — rice and beansprouts was our daily staple — so my brother and I often could not resist stuffing ourselves with spiced rice cakes, fish cake soup, or fried vegetables.

Returning home from one such illicit outing, we were confronted by my mother, who asked us to explain that day's Sunday school lesson. I felt my heart pounding in my chest. I was ready to confess, when Jin smilingly began to recount some Bible story he recalled from a previous week. I was amazed at how convincing he was, but we were both chastened by such a close call. We decided not to take any more chances. The next week we began faithful attendance at Sunday school.

The church itself was one of several buildings on a very large piece of property in Seoul. We passed through an ornate security gate and into a large courtyard. We left our shoes on a rack inside the front door.

I loved to wait in the entrance hall to watch the Moon children come down from their living quarters upstairs. Mrs. Moon would lead them down the staircase, all of them neat and attractive in expensive clothes laundered by one of the church sisters. Mrs. Moon herself was so young and beautiful that it was hard for a little girl not to admire this queenly woman. We all called her Amonim, the Korean word for Mother.

The Reverend and Mrs. Moon would eventually have thirteen children, but there were not so many when I was small. Je Jin, their eldest daughter, was five years my senior. Hyo Jin, the eldest boy, was four years older than I. A girl, In Jin, was born less than a year before me. Heung Jin was born the same year as I, and Un Jin, his sister, was born the year after. The Moons' son Kook Jin was four years younger than I. The Moons' other children were born after they moved to America in 1971.

I admired the Moon children. We all did. We coveted their beautiful mother and powerful father. We were taught to accept the special treatment they received from adults trying to curry favor with the Reverend Moon. We tried to maneuver one of them into our Sunday school groupings because each week we were told that whichever group contributed the most money to the offering would be rewarded. Having one of the Moon children in your group was an obvious asset. The rest of us were poor, but each week the Moon children came to Sunday school grasping crisp new bills to place in the collection plate.

Those bills made a lasting impression on me. I collected shiny Korean coins when I was a little girl. I would select only the shiniest ones, polish them even brighter, and bring them to church on Sundays as my special offering. I did not have much, but I would give the best of what I had to God and the Reverend Moon. When I had children of my own, I continued this childhood habit, searching my purse for the cleanest, newest dollar bills for them to offer up to God.

In Sunday school we learned not only about the *Divine Principle* and the revelations of the Reverend Moon. We heard stories and parables, much like the Bible stories told to children in mainstream Christian religions. However, our stories did not have Jesus as their central figure but Sun Myung Moon. We listened to accounts of his spiritual struggle to establish our religion; we heard tales of his suffering and persecution at the hands of nonbelievers. We were taught that he was a historic figure who carried the burden of fallen man on his strong shoulders. We could not imagine a holier or braver leader than Sun Myung Moon.

We admired the True Children with a similar reverence. We memorized the names and accomplishments of all the Moon children. We added the respectful term *Nim* to their first names when we addressed them. Their academic and artistic accomplishments and their higher level of being were offered to us as evidence of their superiority. We came as close to worshiping them as imaginable.

There was a hierarchy even among ourselves. The Blessed Children of the original three disciples were on a plane by themselves, followed by those of us who were offspring of the next thirty-three couples. Among all of our parents there was fierce competition to push forward their children as prospective brides and grooms for the next generation of Moons. One's status in the church was directly related to one's relationship with the Reverend and Mrs. Moon. To become an in-law was to ensure your family a place in the inner circle.

For those children whose parents had not been blessed, the church could be a cruel place. My brother was near tears relating an incident one Sunday in which a young boy, a non-blessed child, put his bus ticket in the offering plate, only to have it rejected by an insensitive adult, who chastised the boy for his foolishness. Jin was horrified. It was clear that the bus ticket was the boy's most valuable possession.

As children, we rarely had any interaction with the Reverend Moon himself. We saw him on Sundays and on church holidays, and there were many of those. Parents' Day. Children's Day. Day of All Things. God's Day. True Parents' Birthday. Parents' Day commemorates the marriage of Sun Myung Moon and Hak Ja Han, a perfect union that we believed restored Eden and created the foundation for the establishment of Heaven on earth. Children's Day, on October 1, celebrates our connection to the True Parents as children of God. The Day of All Things symbolizes man's dominion over the rest of creation. God's Day is January 1, the first day of the new year, when we recommit ourselves to the Reverend Moon's mission.

Music and food always played a central role in church festivals. Children were expected to entertain the adults, who would have laid out fruit and prepared foods on elaborate offering tables before the Reverend and Mrs. Moon. I dreaded being selected to perform for the Reverend Moon. I was still very shy and there was no disguising the fact that I had a terrible singing voice. In the fourth grade, I was chosen with two other Blessed Children, girlfriends of mine, to sing for the Reverend and Mrs. Moon before the entire congregation. We were terrified, which not did help our performance. It is hard for a child to be calm when she is face to face with the man she believes is an emissary on earth from God himself.

That same year, my parents began sending me to private school. By then we could afford to rent a modest house, but our family was by no means financially secure. In Korea education is a parent's highest priority. My mother and father thought nothing of going without basic comforts to ensure that their seven children received the best education possible. We had few family vacations, but I had piano lessons every day.

Their commitment to education did not mean, however, that my parents always paid the tuition bill on time. One afternoon our teacher asked several of us to remain after class. Payment was overdue. The teacher intended to visit each of our homes to collect the money. I was too ashamed to let my teacher and classmates see the shabby house where we were living, so I took them to my father's office instead.

Industry, the Reverend Moon teaches, is the foundation upon which God's kingdom will be built. He now controls a business empire that includes food processing, fisheries, manufacturing, computers, pharmaceuticals, shipbuilding, and electronics. Il Hwa was the first building block of that empire.

Il Hwa is a health company that produces more than forty pharmaceutical products in four modern manufacturing plants in Korea. It bottles carbonated springwater and a popular soft drink and markets ten different kinds of ginseng products. My father created Il Hwa from nothing. By the time I led my teacher and classmates to his office, my father was presiding over a very successful company. I could see they were impressed and I basked in my father's success.

My father was wiser than many of the Reverend Moon's ardent early followers. He committed himself to the church, but he also completed his education. He did not use his pharmaceutical degree during a decade of street-corner witnessing and church preaching, but in 1971 the Reverend Moon handed him five hundred dollars and told him the church should develop and manufacture ginseng products. The Reverend Moon had been told of the popularity of ginseng in

Japan, where the church was expanding its influence. A Japanese member advised him, correctly as it turned out, that there would be a market in Korea as well.

My father had never actually seen the ginseng root, though he knew that for centuries the perennial herb had been credited by those in the East with extraordinary curative and restorative powers. Ginseng was believed to retard aging, promote sexual virility, and boost energy.

He began the most profitable pharmaceutical company in Korea with a trip to the local market to get a look at what all the fuss was about. For the next ten years, I barely saw my father as he worked to build Il Hwa into a corporate giant specializing in Korean ginseng products including tea, capsules, extract, and beverages. He was gone when I woke up in the morning and he was still at work when I went to sleep at night.

My father transformed an idea into a major moneymaking enterprise for Sun Myung Moon. One of Il Hwa's products, McCol, is a soft drink almost as popular as Coca-Cola in Korea. Il Hwa's McCol and Ginseng-Up and its bottled mineral water have made the company Korea's largest soft drink manufacturer, with 62 percent of the market share and exports to more than thirty countries.

My father's impetus for creating McCol had as much to do with serving the poor as building profits for Il Hwa. The main ingredient of McCol is barley. Its popularity — Sun Myung Moon drinks it even in America — created a market for barley farmers, who live on subsistence earnings in Korea. The son of a farmer, my father toiled not for earthly riches but for heavenly reward. The riches went to Sun Myung Moon.

3

The Little Angels Art School is one of the finest schools for the creative and performing arts in South Korea. It is owned and operated by the Unification Church, but there are no overt signs of the primary and secondary school's connection to the Reverend Sun Myung Moon. Most of the teachers and the majority of students are not Moonies. Religion is not part of the curriculum.

Like so many institutions run by the Reverend Moon around the world, the Little Angels school downplays its relationship with a religious sect that is still deeply distrusted, even in its founder's homeland.

I entered Little Angels in the sixth grade, joining my older brother, Jin, on the sprawling campus, which then housed classes for students in grades seven through twelve. It has since expanded to include the elementary grades.

The school is on the outskirts of Seoul, about fifteen miles from our home. Jin and I would leave our house at 7:00 A.M. to catch the no. 522 city bus. The buses were always crowded with adults on their way to work and students laden with heavy schoolbags. Four or five buses would routinely pass us by, too packed to pick up even two extra passengers. We would pray for the chance to court suffocation if only a bus would stop.

Arriving late was not tolerated at Little Angels. A tardy student would be forced to sit on a concrete bench outside the principal's office with her arms raised above her head for thirty minutes. She would then be required to write a letter of apology to her teacher and classmates for the disruption her late arrival had caused.

On the way to and from the bus stop, Jin insisted I walk several paces behind him. Being seen with one's little sister is no less a humiliation for an adolescent boy in Seoul than in the rest of the world. I willingly obliged. I treated my brother with a formal respect that my nonchurch friends found both curious and amusing. When I spoke to him, I even used the form of address Korean children reserve for adults.

In many ways, my relationship with my brother replicated the one between my parents. Korea's is a rigid, patriarchal culture. My father was a gentle man but he was no egalitarian. He was the undisputed head of our household. His position was reinforced by the teachings of the Unification Church. A marriage is one of mutual respect, but the wife is in the "object" position to her husband just as mankind is in the "object" position to God. I never questioned the balance of power between my mother and father, and I unconsciously modeled my behavior toward my brother on their example.

By the time I was in middle school, the Reverend Moon and his family had moved to the United States. He was directed by God to move to America in 1971, he told his followers, because the United States was on the verge of a moral collapse similar to that which destroyed Rome in the first century.

He went to America to save it from itself. He went preaching his own brand of rabid anti-Communism and moral fundamentalism. He conducted rallies across the United States and found a following among alienated youth caught in the American "generation gap," young people out of step with both their parents and their peers. Their entrée into the Unification Church was often through CARP — the Collegiate Association for the Research of Principles.

CARP was established in the United States in 1973, at the height of protests against American expansion of the war in Vietnam into Cambodia and Laos. The Reverend Moon's dire warnings of the threat of Communism fell largely on deaf ears among American students incensed by their own country's imperialism. CARP recruiters targeted the idealistic and the lonely on college campuses. Students too conservative or apolitical to find common cause with the antiwar movement often found a mission in CARP.

Typical of the membership were the dozens of fresh-faced, neatly dressed young people who staged a day of prayer and fasting on the sidewalk outside the White House in support of President Richard M. Nixon during the Watergate hearings. They held signs that said Forgive, Love, Unite. They were there, on the Washington Mall, on the fringes of antiwar demonstrations, extolling the value of patriotism and the courage of President Nixon in the face of his godless critics.

When CARP members in the United States were not offering encouragement to an embattled president, they were selling flowers on campus, on street corners, in airports, at shopping centers, to raise money for the Reverend Sun Myung Moon and his divine mission.

"The victory of the Allied side in World War II was not an end in itself. From the providential point of view, it had the purpose of preparing America and the world for the Second Coming of the Messiah," Sun Myung Moon has written. "What has happened? The United States did not grasp such a vision. For 40 years, this country has been drifting down the path of self-indulgence, fun and destruction. Drugs have infiltrated the whole country; young people have been corrupted and turn more and more toward delinquency; free sex has become a way of life. But this has not been limited to the United States. As the leader of the free world, the United States has infected the world with its ills. Unless something stops this trend, this nation and the whole world are destined to collapse."

The man who could prevent the Apocalypse, of course, was Sun Myung Moon. To that end, the Reverend Moon himself settled with his growing family into a mansion in the quaint village of Tarrytown, in the Hudson River valley of New York. In 1972 he purchased twenty-two acres in Westchester County for $850,000. The Belvedere Estate was one of the area's architectural gems. The stucco mansion was built in 1920 with sixteen bedrooms, six large public rooms for living and dining, ten full bathrooms, a commercial-sized kitchen, and a full basement. The mansion looked out over rolling lawns, ancient trees, and an artificial one-acre pond, complete with wooden bridge and waterfall. There was a swimming pool and tennis courts and breathtaking views of the Hudson River from the quarry-tiled second-floor sundeck.

Five other buildings stood on the property, including a carriage house that was only slightly smaller than the mansion, with ten bedrooms and three full baths and ten public rooms. There was a five-bedroom wood-frame cottage built in 1735, a gardener's cottage, an artist studio, and a recreation building, plus a four-thousand-square-foot garage and three large greenhouses.

A year later the Reverend Moon purchased a second, eighteen-acre estate not far from Belvedere for $566,150. The centerpiece of the property was a three-story brick mansion with twelve bedrooms, seven bathrooms, a living room, dining room, den, kitchen, and enormous tiled solarium on the west side of the house. The Reverend Moon christened the place East Garden when he and his family took up residence. The Moons retained a private suite of rooms in Belvedere but used that estate primarily to host guests and church functions.

Small buildings dotted the rustic East Garden estate overlooking the Hudson River. A security booth guarded the entrance on Sunnyside Lane, and nearby was a gatehouse with two bedrooms, a bathroom, a living room, and a kitchen, plus a small basement. Just up the hill from the mansion was a lovely stone house with two bedrooms, a bathroom, living room, dining room, den, and kitchen. It was known as Cottage House.

New York was the base of the Reverend Moon's operations, but he still made frequent visits to Korea. When he did, he or one of his top aides would sometimes visit the Little Angels Art School. It was always an occasion for rejoicing as much for the interruption of regular class time as for the chance to see the man some of us considered the new Messiah and all of us knew to be the school's wealthy benefactor.

Korean schools are much like those in Japan and throughout the Pacific Rim. The emphasis is on rote memorization and repetitive drills. By the end of elementary school, I could do advanced mathematics but I could not think critically. It was not a skill that was either taught or valued. Children's minds were considered empty vessels to be filled with knowledge. We were clay to be molded, sculptures to be shaped. This was as true of our moral as of our intellectual development. The educational system, no different at Little Angels school than elsewhere in Korea, stressed deference to authority. It prized consensus and conformity, obedience and acceptance. It prepared me perfectly for life in an authoritarian religion that did not tolerate dissent.

Because I was a disciplined child, academics and music came easily to me. I was a good student by Korean standards. I studied piano with a dutifulness but a lack of fire that I knew pained my mother's heart. I had not inherited her passion for the instrument. I won school piano competitions in the third and sixth grades, but the concert stage was my mother's dream, not mine.

In November 1980 we were pleased to learn that the daily school routine would be broken by a visit from Bo Hi Pak, one of the Reverend Moon's close advisers, to Little Angels. By then the Reverend Moon had become a darling of conservative Republicans in the United States. He had mastered the art of the photo opportunity, having his picture taken with as many prominent world leaders as he could engineer. Those photographs were presented to us as concrete evidence of Father's growing influence in the world.

That day, at Little Angels, Bo Hi Pak was extolling Father's influence on the outcome of the recent American election. A photograph of President Ronald Reagan displaying a front page of the Moon-owned newspaper, the *News World,* proclaiming his landslide victory flashed overhead as Bo Hi Pak spoke. I can't say I paid much attention to the content of his speech. I was thirteen years old, an eighth-grade student. International politics did not interest me. What I knew of America had less to do with politics than with fashion and music, movies and pop culture.

My attention was diverted during his speech by the chattering of my best friend, Hae Sam Hyung, in the next seat. Hae Sam's parents had been part of a group of seventy-two couples who received the marriage Blessing soon after my own parents. "You don't know it yet, but you are going to be matched to Hyo Jin Nim," she whispered while Bo Hi Pak droned on. I stifled a laugh. "That's ridiculous," I said. How would she know such a thing? There were always rumors about who would be chosen to marry the True Children, but those decisions would be made by the Reverend Moon, not by girls giggling in the school auditorium.

Two years later the idea still seemed ridiculous. I had never said more than a few words to Hyo Jin Moon in my life. There were many Blessed Children his own age who would make more suitable marriage partners for a nineteen-year-old True Child than a fifteen-year-old girl like me. I did not know Hyo Jin well but I had heard enough to know he was the black sheep of the Moon family. He was in elementary school when the Moons moved to America. He had been a diligent, if reluctant, student in Korea. Peter Kim, the Reverend Moon's personal assistant, was assigned to tutor the young heir apparent. Hyo Jin vowed that when he went to America, he would have more freedom than he had known in Seoul.

The move to the United States was not an easy transition for him. Life was even more isolated in the Moon compound in Tarrytown than it had been in Seoul. At home the Moon children were left to the care of church elders and baby-sitters. At school they were the ultimate outsiders.

They were sent to the private Hackley School, where their identities as Moonies subjected them to teasing or outright scorn. Hyo Jin was expelled from Hackley in middle school for bringing a BB gun to school and shooting at several classmates. Hyo Jin claimed the headmaster thought him both honest and amusing because he admitted that his reason for doing it was nothing more complicated than that it was fun. He was expelled nonetheless. He had been terrified to face his father after his expulsion. Had the Reverend Moon punished his son decisively back then, he might have saved us all a lot of grief. Instead the Reverend Moon treated Hyo Jin as if he were the victim of religious persecution. It was part of a lifetime pattern of evading his responsibility for Hyo Jin Moon.

The Reverend and Mrs. Moon were absentee parents, promoting the church around the world and ignoring their own children at home. Hyo Jin was an especially difficult challenge. As their oldest son, he would be expected to inherit Father's place as head of the church. But a long-haired rock guitarist with a chip on his shoulder was not what the Reverend Moon had in mind for a successor.

After Hyo Jin was expelled from Hackley, the Reverend Moon sent him to live with Bo Hi Pak, one of his original disciples, in McLean, a wealthy Virginia suburb outside of Washington, D.C. It was the Reverend Moon's theory that his followers were responsible for rearing the Messiah's children. The Reverend Moon, after all, was responsible for the care of the world. It was an odd theory for a man who claimed to be the model father of the ideal family, and no one felt the dichotomy more than Hyo Jin Moon.

Hyo Jin's behavior only deteriorated in Washington. In a large public school, there were fistfights and worse. It was in Washington that he was first introduced to illegal drugs. "Going to Washington was a great excitement for me, to leave East Garden," Hyo Jin told church members in a speech in 1988.

Father told me not to associate with outside kids but I wanted to associate with outside people. I felt this was a chance for me to seek friends. I didn't think, didn't care, about what Father wanted. I wanted my own friends.

After I went to Washington, I started getting into drugs. I didn't want to be pressured by bullies anymore.

*When you're in high school, fists work. I started taking
martial arts. I didn't want to take anything from anyone.
In school, they go around in packs. But kids who had control were the strongest. When they saw me, they saw
"gooks," so I had a lot of fights. The more I fought, the
more I won. Then kids wanted to become friends. My
name was notorious.*

A frustrated Reverend Moon sent Hyo Jin back to Korea for
high school, hoping that the supervision of church elders in
his own culture would straighten him out. It did not work out
that way. Hyo Jin was quite a sight in the corridors of Little
Angels, with his long, dirty hair and his tight blue jeans. He
started a rock 'n' roll band and he cultivated a reputation for
defiance.

It was hard enough to belong to a mistrusted religious sect
as an adolescent. Hyo Jin's appearance and behavior made it
more difficult for the rest of us. We were embarrassed by him
in front of nonmembers. Our own musical tastes ran more to
the classical. To compound matters, he was openly contemptu-
ous of Father's strict code of conduct. Everyone in school knew
Hyo Jin smoked cigarettes, had girlfriends, and drank alcohol.
Some whispered that he used illegal drugs. He never actually
finished his course of study at Little Angels; years later the
school simply mailed him a diploma.

There was enormous competition among the thirty-six
Blessed Couples, the original members of the church, to have
one of their daughters matched to Hyo Jin Moon. One's standing in the church was directly related to one's proximity to Sun
Myung Moon. To be an in-law was to be as close as a member
could get. Mr. and Mrs. Young Whi Kim, for example, expected
their eldest daughter, Un Sook Kim, to be matched to Hyo Jin
because of their status as one of the original Three Couples.

Young Whi Kim was then the president of the Unification Church in Korea. The irony was that even those couples who wanted their daughters to marry Hyo Jin discouraged their children, of both genders, from associating with him because of his taste for drugs and sex and rock 'n' roll.

As for Hyo Jin, he wanted nothing to do with being matched for "spiritual" reasons. "When I went to Korea, I started going with many girls," he confessed in his 1988 speech to members.

> *I really loved one in particular and wanted to marry her. Her parents liked the idea; they thought Father had a lot of money. They encouraged both of us, invited me to their home. They were nice to me. We became very close, almost lived together. I had sex with her. I wanted to do everything in my power to stay with her. I wanted to be matched with her or nobody else. After school, I would sleep over at her house and she at my house, all through high school.*
>
> *I drank a bottle of whiskey a day. If I didn't have money, I would buy corn whiskey, cheap and potent. I had to be drunk all the time. . . . I touched bottom. I was listening to my heart cry. I started suffocating. I wanted to kill myself. How could I face Father. I thought the best way was to disappear, then I would have no burden. Many times I sat with a gun pointed to my head, practiced what it would be like. I only cared about my physical body. I was worse than other kids. I was so physical and selfish. I didn't care how I affected other people. That's how I grew up.*

What did I know of boys, never mind bad boys like Hyo Jin Moon? Girls and boys attend separate schools in Korea. At Little Angels, an arts school that attracted an overwhelmingly female student body, there were a few boys, but they did not mix much with the girls. Most boys were members of the Unification Church and, as such, were not allowed to date.

My only encounter with a boy as a teenager had left me with the overriding impression that the opposite sex was an annoyance to be avoided. A boy my age would hang round outside our church on Sundays when I was thirteen, waiting for me to emerge. He was not a member of the Unification Church but lived in the neighborhood. He must have spotted me going to and from the bus stop. Every week he would try to strike up a conversation and every week I would ignore him. I was delighted when we moved to a new church building in another neighborhood. I would be rid of him. But there he was, that first Sunday, waiting for me outside the new church. I never knew his name; eventually he gave up his pursuit.

Among my friends at Little Angels, there was the usual innocent preteen talk about which boys ranked among the cutest. I would just listen. Having begun school so early, I was a year younger than most of my classmates. I was smaller physically, too, still a pretty little girl when my friends were flowering into graceful young women.

We knew we'd all be matched someday by the Reverend Moon to the men we would marry. We assumed that eventuality was years away, after we had completed our studies at the university and begun our lives as adults. The median age for a woman to marry in Korea is twenty-five. When the time came, I knew that I would accept the Reverend Moon's choice for me. My parents expected it. I would obey. I gave the prospect of marriage little thought because it would not happen for years and I would have little to say about it when it did.

In my deference to my elders in the matter of marriage, I was not so different from other young women in my culture. Arranged marriages are still commonplace in Korea, where they have been the traditional means of maintaining or elevating a family's social status for centuries. Many young people taken with Western influences do marry for love, but most Koreans remain skeptical that romance provides a solid foundation for family life. Even lovers who choose one another as marriage partners often confirm their decision by visiting a fortune-teller.

It would be hard to overstate my naïveté as a fifteen-year-old girl. My mother had explained menstruation to me when I was ten. It was the only time that she and I even came close to discussing sex. The atmosphere in the room that day was so heavy, her discomfort so pronounced, we might have been discussing a fatal disease. I remember squirming as I sat on the floor, wanting to relieve her embarrassment more than I wanted to learn any womanly secrets she had to impart.

The truth is, I had little curiosity about the whispers and giggles I heard in the school corridors between boys and girls. I made no effort to decipher the punch lines of jokes I did not understand. Once, on the bus, I stood next to a teacher with a reputation for bothering girls at school. He grabbed my hand and stared at me throughout the ride. I tried to pull my hand away but he was too strong. My fingers turned red, then white, in his tight grasp. I thought it was odd, but it never occurred to me there might be some sexual threat in his advances.

During that assembly at school, I had laughed about my friend's prediction of a marriage between me and Hyo Jin Moon, though I did tell my mother when I returned home. She looked surprised, but we never spoke of it again. One day we would be distracted not by rumor but by a real match in the Hong household.

When I first entered Little Angels Art School, older girls would whisper when I walked past, "That's Jin's little sister," and pride would make my chest swell. I basked in his reflected glory. Jin was the most popular boy in school. He was handsome, smart, the class president. It was an honor to be his sister.

At school more than one girl wrote him silly love notes. He blushed at their attention, but he was a good boy. He took the moral code of the church seriously. We were forbidden to have anything other than a sisterly or brotherly relationship with members of the opposite sex. We were not allowed to date. We were to keep ourselves pure until Father decided it was time for us to marry.

When Jin was seventeen and I barely fifteen, I could sense there was something about to happen in our house. The whole atmosphere was charged. There was an undercurrent of tension and excitement, although my parents said nothing to us children. The Moons were living in the United States at the time, but rumors were rife that they were looking among the Blessed Children in Korea for a groom for their oldest child, Je Jin. Everyone expected the groom to be chosen from among the sons of the earliest disciples, Young Whi Kim or Hyo Won Eu. Their sons, Jin Kun Kim and Jin Seung Eu, were friends of my older brother.

One day, after school, I was surprised to see both of my parents at home, outfitted in their best clothes. I could hear Jin, dressing in his room. He emerged in a new suit, with his hair slicked back like a Korean businessman's. My brothers and sisters and I gasped. He looked so grown up. My parents offered no explanation and, characteristically, we did not ask. It was not until they returned from their mysterious errand with Jin hours later that they told the six of us that our brother had been matched to Je Jin Moon. He was to be married to the daughter of the Messiah. He was to become a member of the True Family of God.

I was so proud. Jin was special and I would be special, too, because Jin was my brother. My pride gave way to sadness when I thought about his actually leaving our family. He was so young, and he was so much a part of my life. Ours was not so religious a household that we did not sometimes bend the rigid rules of the church. Gambling was forbidden by the Reverend Moon as a corrupting influence, but my brothers and sisters and I often played a Korean card game called Wha Tu. The losers sometimes would buy the winner a lunch of black Chinese noodles, delivered to our front door straight from the restaurant by a boy on a bicycle. Would that end now, without Jin?

With Jin gone, who would help me with the art classes in which I struggled so? My sadness paled, though, next to Choong Sook's, who faced the prospect of me as the eldest sibling in the Hong family. I had not learned from the example of my brother, who exerted authority among us by the goodness of his character. I took the more direct approach to power. I am ashamed to say that I treated Choong Sook, who was two years younger than I, like my personal servant. My grandmother even called me Choon Hyang after the lady in a famous Korean love story and my sister Hyang Dan, after the lady's maid.

We were stunned to learn that the wedding of Je Jin and Jin would be held the next day. We had all been taught the significance of the marriage Blessing, its central role in our spiritual lives and the need to approach that moment with due deliberation. Je Jin and Jin could not possibly have had time to do that. It was as though the Reverend Moon were marrying off his daughter between stops on one of his world tours.

Marriage is at the center of Unification doctrine. The Reverend Moon teaches that, because Jesus was crucified before he could marry and sire sinless children, the Kingdom of Heaven on Earth had not been opened to mankind. It is the Reverend Moon's role as Lord of the Second Advent to complete the work Jesus left undone. The Reverend Moon's marriage to Hak Ja Han in 1960 began a new era, one that the Unification Church calls the Completed Testament Era. This perfect couple, the True Parents, produced the first True Family by having children born free of original sin. The rest of humankind can become part of this sinless legacy only by receiving the marriage Blessing from the Unification Church.

The Reverend and Mrs. Moon would complete Jesus' mission to restore humanity by reenacting the role of Adam and Eve in the Garden of Eden, this time without sin. Since the Unification Church teaches that the Fall was an act of sexual misconduct, the Reverend Moon will restore humanity through a "principled," monogamous marriage. Other couples could be freed from the satanic blood lineage of Adam and Eve — original sin — only by receiving the Blessing and becoming one with the True Family.

Before and after receiving the Blessing, the church requires a couple to participate in several complex rituals, most of which were waived in the case of Je Jin Moon and Jin Hong. The Reverend Moon teaches that three years should elapse between the initial Matching Ceremony and the actual consummation of the marriage in what is called the Three Day Ceremony. In this case, there was no Matching Ceremony, no Holy Wine Ceremony, no Indemnity Ceremony, no Three Day Ceremony, even though the Reverend Moon teaches that each very specific ritual has profound theological meaning.

Theoretically, to become engaged in the Unification Church, one must have been a member for three years, one must have recruited three new members, and one must have made the required financial contribution to the Indemnity Fund. This payment symbolizes Unification teaching that all of humanity shares in the debt owed for the betrayal of Jesus and that we must all pay for this collective sin.

In the Matching Ceremony, a couple is called before the Reverend and Mrs. Moon, who explain the significance of the Blessing and ask them to adjourn to a separate room to decide whether to accept the match. As the church grew, the Blessing Committee was formed to rule on matches, but in the early days and in the case of his family, the Reverend Moon made the matches himself.

The Holy Wine Ceremony is usually held the same day as the Matching Ceremony. Facing the man, the woman drinks half a cup of blessed wine and then passes the cup to the man. The woman drinks first to symbolize Eve, the first to sin and now the first to be restored to grace. The few drops left in the cup are sprinkled on a Holy Handkerchief to be used after the Blessing at the Three Day Ceremony. After a couple receives the Blessing, there is a private Indemnity Ceremony in which the husband and wife each ritually and symbolically "beat" Satan out of the other with sticks.

The Three Day Ceremony is the consummation of the marriage. In most situations the couple is not to have sex for the first three years of their married life. When they do, they must follow a detailed pattern of sex acts prescribed by the Reverend Moon. On the morning of the third day, the couple joins together in prayer. They then bathe and wipe their bodies with the Holy Handkerchief, which has been dipped first in wine and then in cold water. The woman takes the superior position for the first two nights, symbolizing a restored Eve bringing grace first to Satan and then to the fallen Adam. On the third night, the man assumes the superior position, symbolizing the restored Adam and Eve fulfilling the mission God had intended for them at the dawn of creation.

This was the first wedding of a True Child of the Reverend and Mrs. Moon. The absence of many of the Blessing-related rituals was something of a shock. The whole proceeding had the air of a shotgun wedding. What was the rush? I wondered. Why was church doctrine being set aside to marry Je Jin and Jin almost literally overnight? Much later I would learn that the rules did not apply to the Moon family. All had sex immediately after the Blessing, if they had not already had sex before.

My siblings and I were not thinking about that as we sat at the back of the church. Our parents were up front with the Moons and the bride and groom. We could barely see. We all missed a day of school to attend the ceremony. Je Jin was beautiful in a white wedding gown and my brother was more handsome than ever, like the plastic groom on top of a wedding cake. We had to strain to hear them exchange their vows.

> *Do you, as mature men and women, who are to consummate the ideal of the creation of God, pledge to become an eternal husband and wife?*
>
> *Do you pledge that you shall become a true husband and wife, and raise your children to live up to the will of God, and educate them to become responsible leaders in front of your family, all humankind, and Almighty God?*
>
> *Do you pledge that, centering on True Parents, you shall inherit the tradition of family unity, and pass this proud tradition down to the future generations of your family and all humankind?*
>
> *Do you pledge that, centering upon the ideal of creation, you will inherit the will of God and the True Parents, establish God's traditions of the love of children, brother and sister, husband and wife and parents [the Four Great Realms of the Heart] and the love of grandparents, parents and children [the Three Great Kingships] and love the people of the world as God and True Parents do, and*

ultimately consummate the ideal family which is the build-ing block of the Kingdom of God on earth and in Heaven?

As they made their vows, I saw Hyo Jin Moon across the room, his long hair spilling over the collar of his dark suit. He was taking photographs of the ceremony but he looked sour and angry. I was mystified. Why would anyone look so un-happy at a wedding? It is only in retrospect that I recognize the familiar pattern: I suspect Hyo Jin was sulking because he was not the center of attention.

After the wedding a dinner reception was held in a large ballroom in the Palace Hotel. Our parents were there with all of the Moons, but we, Jin's brothers and sisters, were not invited to attend. One of my uncles took the six of us to dinner in a hotel restaurant, but we were heartbroken to be excluded from our brother's wedding celebration. This was a Moon affair; the Hongs were clearly secondary players.

Soon after the wedding, the Moons and Je Jin flew back to America. Je Jin was a student at Smith, the prestigious women's college in Massachusetts. Jin moved into the Reverend Moon's house in Seoul with Hyo Jin and a large household staff. He still had a year of high school to complete, and it was not easy to obtain a visa to travel to the United States.

Living with Hyo Jin was difficult for my brother. Hyo Jin had been raised as a prince and he acted like one, leaving his clothes on the floor to be picked up by the sisters and ordering the household staff around as if they were his personal slaves. He brought his girlfriends home to the house to have sex. He filled the place with cigarette smoke. Jin was in an impossible position. He disapproved of Hyo Jin's behavior but he could not criticize the son of the Messiah. Hyo Jin was a True Child; Jin had merely married one.

My own life resumed its routine after my brother's marriage. I would see him at Little Angels, but we shared little more than passing conversation. He studied all the time. Regular school hours end at 3:00 P.M. but older students often stay until 9:00 P.M. to prepare for university entrance exams. Besides, Jin was on another, higher plane now. He was no longer my brother but a member of the True Family. I missed him terribly.

When I thought about my own future, and I rarely did, I envisioned many more years of study. I never missed a day of school. I was becoming more diligent at the piano. Maybe I would fulfill my mother's dream and become a pianist after all. Maybe I would marry another pianist and we could play concerts together around the world. Hadn't a fortune-teller once told my mother that I would be very famous one day, married to an important man?

Such thoughts were all in the realm of girlish fantasy. I followed the rigid code of the Unification Church. I was aghast in class one afternoon to see my seatmate applying eye makeup. She was not a member of the church. She had a date after school, she said. I was at once fascinated and horrified.

Six months after the Blessing of Je Jin and Jin, in November 1981, the Little Angels Art School staged a production of traditional Korean music and dance to celebrate the opening of a new theater. The school had expanded steadily since it was founded by the Reverend Moon in 1974. The adjoining performance arts center was home to the Little Angels folk ballet that the Reverend Moon had established in 1965. The Little Angels, a troupe of seven- to fifteen-year-old girls, have performed around the world for heads of state and royalty in Japan and Great Britain.

I had no such performing talent. For the theater dedication, I was given a small role in the chorus. I was a nervous wreck as

I waited backstage with the other girls, my hair pulled back into a tight single braid, my beautiful costume no disguise, I knew, for my terrible voice.

The conductor was lining us up to go onstage when I heard my name called. The principal was suddenly at my side. "Your mother has sent a car for you," she said. "You must go and change."

I returned to the dressing room to replace my costume with my school uniform. I stepped into the navy blue plaid skirt, buttoned my white blouse, and slipped on my blue blazer. I put on the gray wool coat with the black fur collar that was part of our winter uniform, grabbed my red hat and red book bag, and hurried to the waiting sedan. I got into the rear seat of the car with no idea where I was being taken. It speaks volumes about my level of obedience that I did not ask.

I had never been to the Reverend Moon's private residence. It was an enormous house with an elaborate front gate that led to a large courtyard. A sister led me to an ornate dining room. My mother was already there. Three chairs were lined up on either side of the rectangular dining table. The Reverend Moon sat at the head; Mrs. Moon sat to his right. Beside her sat a woman I did not recognize. Next to her was Mrs. Young Whi Kim. My mother was seated opposite Mrs. Moon. My mother smiled and gestured for me to sit beside her. I kept my eyes downcast, focusing on the patterns of light and shadow cast by the large crystal chandelier on the white linen tablecloth.

My head remained bowed as the kitchen sisters served course after course of the dinner meal. I was too scared to eat the rice or soup or kimchi or seafood or meat. I moved the food around my plate and prayed no one would take notice of me.

It struck me that Mrs. Moon seemed to be in very good spirits. There was a lot of laughter, but I did not focus on the conversation until I suddenly realized they were talking about me. The woman at the table whom I had not recognized was staring at me. She was commenting on my forehead and the shape of my head. She was delighted that my hair had been pulled back for the performance at school. It gave her the opportunity to examine my ears more closely. I could feel my face flush as she cataloged the positive characteristics of my ears: earlobes that were long and fat, a shape that was well proportioned. All this meant longevity and good fortune.

I felt panic as my mother rose to clear her plate as the dinner gathering was breaking up. I followed her through the swinging doors into the kitchen, where the sisters laughed and smiled, obviously pleased by something more than my ears. On the way home, it was clear that my mother was pleased, too, by the day's events, but she offered no explanation for our visit to the Moon household. If she did not tell me, I knew it was not my place to ask.

The next day I was surprised when my mother sent me to a hairdresser to have my long straight black hair curled. I was even more confused to see that she had laid out her own blue suit for me to wear. It would make me look more grown up, she said. I returned with my parents to the Moons' house. This time a large crowd had assembled. All the leaders of the church were there. I seemed to be attracting a lot of attention. Everyone smiled at me. My mother's pretty suit, I thought. A photographer kept taking my picture. There was a mountainous amount of food.

My parents and I were soon called into a room to meet privately with the Reverend and Mrs. Moon. My parents sat on floor pillows across from the Moons. I bowed and knelt before them on the floor. The Reverend Moon was speaking so softly, I could barely hear him. I kept my head bowed. As I knelt silently before him, the Reverend Moon asked my parents to please give their daughter to the True Family. My mother and father did not look at me when they said yes.

"So that's it," I thought. "I'm being matched." The Reverend Moon asked me no questions. He made no attempt to engage me in conversation, to determine what I was like. He already knew enough. The unfamiliar woman at dinner, it turned out, was a Buddhist spiritualist, a fortune-teller, who assured the Reverend Moon that I would make a perfect match for Hyo Jin. The woman whom I came to think of as the Buddha Lady was not a member of the Unification Church. It never occurred to me or my parents to ask why the Reverend Moon needed to consult a Buddhist fortune-teller for advice if he was the Lord of the Second Advent, in regular, direct communication with God.

Did I want to be matched to his son, Hyo Jin, Father asked. I did not hesitate. This was every Unification girl's dream, to be matched to a member of the True Family. To be Hyo Jin Moon's wife meant I would one day be the Mother of the church. I felt humbled and honored. That Hyo Jin himself was no girl's idea of prince charming did not even occur to me. A Blessing was the uniting of two souls, not just the union of two human beings. God would turn Hyo Jin toward a righteous path, and the Reverend Moon had chosen me as an instrument of that mission. "Yes, Father," I said, lifting my eyes to meet his. "She's prettier than Mother," he said. I pretended not to hear, but I could not help wondering what Mrs. Moon was thinking. I dared not steal a glance at her face.

All my life I had been told I was pretty by my family and my friends. There were girls much more beautiful than I, of course, but I knew I was pleasing to look at and it pleased me to hear the Reverend Moon say as much. I have never known exactly why Sun Myung Moon chose me to marry his eldest son. Maybe he thought I was pretty, a good student from a good family. At the time, that was explanation enough for me. As the years went on, I came to believe that my youth and naïveté were the central reasons for my selection. I was younger than Hak Ja Han was when the Messiah married her. His ideal wife was a girl young and passive enough to submit while he molded her into the woman he wanted. Time would prove that I was young, but not nearly passive enough.

Hyo Jin was waiting in an adjoining room. The Reverend Moon sent me back to see him. Both parties must agree to the Blessing, but it was not as if either of us had any real choice. We knew that the Reverend Moon frowns upon individuals selecting their own partner; matches are to be based on spiritual compatibility, not physical attraction; the Reverend Moon is better equipped than any individual to make that judgment.

I had never been alone with a boy, let alone the son of the Messiah. I bowed and greeted him stiffly as "Hyo Jin Nim." He said I should not use the formal title Nim if we were to be married. He called me to sit by him on the couch. He held my hand. I tried to relax but I was so very shy. We had nothing to say to one another. After a few awkward minutes, Hyo Jin said we should return to his parents.

We went down to the living room, where the Reverend Moon conducted a prayer service. We all held hands. Mrs. Moon took a ruby-and-diamond ring from her own hand and slipped it onto my finger to seal our engagement. The Reverend and Mrs. Moon both cried and expressed their hope that Hyo Jin now would prove himself worthy to be the son of the Messiah.

As my parents and I left for home, my mother hit her head hard as she bent to enter the car. Ours is a superstitious culture. How many times in the years ahead would my mother and I ask each other why we had not seen that bump as a warning sign of the pain to come?

4

I entered the United States illegally on January 3, 1982. In order to obtain a visa, the Unification Church concocted a story about my participation in an international piano competition in New York City.

Had American immigration officials only heard me play, they would have recognized the ruse immediately. A pianist of my limited abilities would not have been among the contestants had such an event actually existed. To lend credence to the claim, the Reverend Sun Myung Moon had the best piano student at Little Angels school accompany me to New York for the same phony recital.

I confess I did not give much thought to the deceit that frigid winter day when my parents and I waved good-bye to my brothers and sisters and left for America. We accepted the Reverend Moon's view that man's laws are secondary to God's plan. By his rationale, a fraudulently obtained visa was no less than an instrument of God's design for my Holy Marriage to Hyo Jin Moon.

The truth is, I had not been thinking much at all in the six weeks since our engagement. Looking back, what I most resembled was a porcelain windup doll. Turn the key and she walks, she talks, she smiles. I was a schoolgirl, overwhelmed by the transformation I had undergone literally overnight. One day I was a child, shooed from the room whenever adults were discussing serious matters. The next day I was a member of the True Family, fumbling for the appropriate response when my elders bowed before me.

After Hyo Jin and his parents returned to America, my mother and I spent weeks shopping for a wardrobe that would match my metamorphosis from girl to woman. Gone were my school uniforms, my T-shirts and blue jeans. My teenage self was buried beneath tailored business suits and conservative sheaths. Awkward though I felt in this new role, I savored the attention. What girl would not revel in a round of dinner parties thrown in her honor? Whose head would not be turned by the solicitations of those so many years her senior?

If there was any hint of the troubles to come, it was in the discomfort I felt in the company of my intended. In December Hyo Jin Moon returned briefly to Korea, without his parents. Our meetings were strained as much by our lack of common interests as by his relentless pressure for sex. My mother had given me several books to read about marriage, but I was still unclear what the sex act actually entailed.

Hyo Jin took me to the Moon family's home in Seoul during his visit and, under the pretext of showing me his room, cornered me by his bed. "Lie down with me," he said. "You can trust me. We'll be married soon." I did as he asked, only to stiffen with fear as his clearly experienced hands groped my body and his fingers fumbled with layer upon layer of my winter clothing. "Touch me here," he instructed, his hands guiding my own along his inner thigh. "Stroke me there."

Sex before marriage is strictly prohibited by the Unification Church. Because Sun Myung Moon teaches that the Fall was a sexual act, incidents of premarital or extramarital sex are considered the most serious sin one can commit. Here I was, a scared and virginal girl of fifteen, having to remind the scion of the Unification Church, the son of the Messiah, that we both risked eternal damnation if I did as he demanded. He seemed more amused than angry at my righteous naïveté. For my part, I believed with all my heart that God had chosen me to guide Hyo Jin away from his sinful path.

I had no idea how difficult that task would be. Even as the Korean Airlines jet landed at Kennedy International Airport in New York, I gave no thought to what my life actually would be like in America, a world away from everything I knew and everyone I loved. Humbled by my selection as Hyo Jin Moon's bride, swept up in events being orchestrated by others, I did not ask myself how a mere mortal would fit into the "divine" family of Sun Myung Moon or how a virtuous girl could tame an older rebellious youth like Hyo Jin Moon.

As we deplaned in New York, I became separated from my parents in the crush of travelers being herded into lines for U.S. customs. The uniformed agent looked annoyed when I handed him my two large suitcases. He spoke brusquely to me, but because I did not speak English, I could not answer his questions. There was a flurry of activity and some shouting before someone came to assist me.

I watched as the customs agent dumped my neatly folded clothes onto the counter, searching the side and back pockets of my luggage. What was he looking for? What would I have?

It did not occur to me that the customs agent had reason to be suspicious. Where was my sheet music for this piano competition? Why had I packed so much for such a brief trip? Wasn't I wearing thousands of dollars' worth of necklaces given to me as engagement gifts in Korea? Hadn't church leaders told me to hide them beneath my sedate brown dress?

I was arriving in the United States at the height of American antipathy toward Sun Myung Moon. He was reviled in the United States as a public menace on the order of the Reverend Jim Jones, the leader of the Peoples' Temple cult who, in 1978, had fed more than nine hundred of his followers cyanide-laced fruit juice in a mass suicide in Guyana. The newspapers in America were full of stories about young people being brainwashed into following Sun Myung Moon. A cottage industry of "deprogrammers" had sprung up across the country, paid by parents to kidnap their children from Unification Church centers and "reeducate" them.

Having been born into the Unification Church, I knew little firsthand about the recruitment techniques that had made the church so controversial. I was skeptical about such melodramatic descriptions as "brainwashing," but it was certainly true that new members were isolated from old friends and family. Church members were encouraged to learn as much as possible about new recruits in order to tailor an individual approach to win him or her over to the Unification Church. Members would "love bomb" new recruits with so much personal attention it is hardly any wonder that vulnerable young people responded so enthusiastically to their new "family."

It was a recruit's old family that usually suspected sinister motives in this all-embracing religious community. The year I came to America, it was not uncommon for travelers to be approached at airports, at traffic signals, or on street corners by young people selling trinkets or flowers for the Unification Church. Begging is hard and humiliating work and followers of Sun Myung Moon did it better than most. Asking for money is easier when you believe your panhandling is going to support the work of the Messiah.

The American government had as many questions about Sun Myung Moon's finances as American parents had about his theology. Senator Robert Dole, the ranking Republican on the Senate Finance Committee, had concluded hearings on the Unification Church with a recommendation that the Internal Revenue Service investigate the tax status of the Reverend Moon and his church. Only a month before my engagement, a federal grand jury in New York had indicted the Reverend Moon, charging him with evading income taxes for 1972 to 1974, as well as conspiracy to avoid taxes. No doubt that indictment had more to do with the scrutiny I received at JFK International Airport than the size of my suitcases did.

I knew none of that then, of course. I knew only that I was coming to America to join the True Family. Hyo Jin Moon paced impatiently outside the customs area. As I emerged, shaken from my ordeal, I looked around for the reassurance of my parents, but Hyo Jin hustled me to the parking area and his black sports car, an engagement gift from his father. He carried a small bouquet of flowers but was so exasperated by the delay he almost forgot to give them to me. My parents would meet us at East Garden, he said. I was too tired to object.

It was a silent, forty-minute drive north from New York City to Westchester County, through the wealthy suburbs where Manhattan's corporate executives and professional elite make their homes in quaint, rural towns along the Hudson River. It was late. It was too dark to see much and I was too tired to care.

I paid more attention as we drove through the black, wrought iron gates. This was East Garden, at last. Hyo Jin acknowledged the guard at the security booth and headed up the long, winding driveway. Even in the dark, I thought I could make out the exact spot on the rolling lawn that I had gazed at reverentially for so many years. In our home in Korea, my family displayed a photograph of the True Family, seated on the emerald green grass of their American estate. I used to stare at that photograph, unshakable in my belief in the perfection of the individuals pictured there. In their expensive clothes, posed in front of their magnificent mansion, they represented the ideal family we prayed to emulate. I treasured that photograph the way other teenagers treasured photographs of rock 'n' roll stars.

The Reverend and Mrs. Moon and the three oldest of their twelve children greeted us at the door. I bowed down to Father and Mother, humbled to be in their home. I listened for the sound of another car as I was led through the enormous foyer into what they called the yellow room, a beautiful solarium. Where were my parents? When would they and the church elders come? Surely I would not have to converse alone with the Reverend and Mrs. Moon!

As I entered the house, I stopped to take off my heavy winter boots. In Korea one never enters a home without first removing one's shoes. It is a sign of respect as well as an act of fastidiousness. Hyo Jin's sister, In Jin, stopped me. I should not keep her parents waiting. In the yellow room, we exchanged pleasantries about my trip. I smiled and said little, keeping my eyes downcast. It is impossible to overstate the level of my nervousness. I had never been alone in the company of the True Family. I was nearly paralyzed by a mixture of fear and reverence. I was relieved to hear the slam of a car door signaling the arrival of my parents.

While our parents conversed downstairs, Hyo Jin took me on a brief tour of the mansion. As large as it was, the house seemed to be bursting with children and their nannies. When I arrived in America, Mrs. Moon was pregnant with her thirteenth child. Most of the little ones and their baby-sitters were asleep that night in their barrackslike quarters on the third floor. Seeing them tucked in their beds made me ache for my own younger brothers and sisters back home in Korea, especially the youngest, Jin Chool, who was six years old.

It was well past midnight when we said good night to the Moons and a driver took my parents and me to Belvedere, the church-owned estate a few minutes from East Garden where guests often stayed. First my parents were shown to a room, then I was escorted down the hall to the most beautiful bedroom I had ever seen. Decorated in shades of pink and cream, the room was fit for a princess. In addition to the queen-sized bed, the room had a living area with a large couch and comfortable armchairs. It had a crystal chandelier and two walk-in closets bigger than some of the rooms we rented in Seoul when I was small. The bathroom was enormous, its original blue-and-white hand-painted tiles retaining the elegance of the 1920s, when the mansion was built.

I had never seen such a room. There was even a television set. I fumbled with the controls, and though I did not understand a single English word, I quickly discerned that I was seeing some kind of advertisement. I wish I had a photograph of my expression when I realized that I was watching a commercial for dog food. Special food for dogs? I was transfixed by the scene of a dog scampering across a kitchen floor to a bowl full of brown nuggets. In Korea, dogs eat table scraps. I fell asleep on my first night in America in a state of wonder — I was living in a country so rich that dogs had their own cuisine!

In the morning a driver returned to take my parents and me to the Moons' breakfast table in the wood-paneled dining room at East Garden. This is where the Reverend Moon conducts his business and church affairs. Every morning leaders come here to report to him in Korean about his financial enterprises around the globe. At the long rectangular dining table, the Reverend Moon decides what projects to fund, what companies to buy, what personnel to promote or demote.

The Moon children do not eat their meals with their parents. They appear at the breakfast table to bow to the Reverend and Mrs. Moon each morning to begin their day. Then they are led away to the kitchen, where they are fed before school or playtime. On this morning, the older children joined their parents and mine for breakfast. I caught sight of the little ones peeking through the kitchen door to steal a glimpse of me, their new sister. I felt warmed by their giggles but shocked to learn that the younger Moon children did not speak Korean.

The Reverend Moon teaches that Korean is the universal language of the Kingdom of Heaven. He has written that "English is spoken only in the colonies of the Kingdom of Heaven! When the Unification Church movement becomes more advanced, the international and official language of the Unification Church shall be Korean; the official conferences will be conducted in Korean, similar to the Catholic conferences, which are conducted in Latin." I knew that members around the world were encouraged to learn Korean, so I was confused by the failure of the Reverend and Mrs. Moon to teach their own children what I had been taught was the language of God.

I was overpowered that morning by the strange smells of an American breakfast. There was bacon and sausage, eggs and pancakes. The sight of all that food made me slightly nauseous. In Korea I was accustomed to a simple morning meal of kimchi and rice. Mrs. Moon had instructed the kitchen sisters to serve papaya, her favorite fruit. She knew I would never have tasted such an exotic delicacy and she kept urging me to try some. She showed me how to sprinkle the fruit with lemon juice to enhance the flavor, but I simply could not eat. She looked displeased. My mother ate the papaya placed before me and praised Mrs. Moon for her excellent choice.

The Reverend Moon sensed my unease. He spoke directly to Hyo Jin: "Nansook is in a strange place, in a foreign country. She does not speak the language or know the customs. This is your home. You must be kind to her." I was so grateful to have my fears acknowledged by the Reverend Moon that I only vaguely noticed that Hyo Jin said nothing in response.

Hyo Jin did come to see me at Belvedere but his few visits were not reassuring. They only reinforced how ill-suited we were to one another. I was afraid of him. He would try to embrace me and I would pull away. I did not know how to be with a boy, let alone with a man I was soon to marry. "Why are you running away from me?" he would ask. How could I tell him what I was too young to understand myself? I was honored to be the spiritual partner of the son of the Messiah but I was not ready to be the wife of a flesh-and-blood man.

I passed through the next four days as if in a series of dream sequences. I moved from scene to scene, numb from exhaustion and the magnitude of unfolding events. I went where I was directed. I did as I was told, concerned only that I make no mistakes that would displease the Reverend and Mrs. Moon.

Mrs. Moon took my mother and me shopping at a suburban mall. I had never seen so many stores. Mrs. Moon gravitated to the most expensive shops. At Neiman-Marcus she selected unflattering, matronly dresses in dark colors for me to try on. She chose bright red or royal blue outfits for herself. I suspect that she resented my youth. She had heard her husband on my engagement day say that I was prettier than she. It was hard for me to imagine a woman as stunning as Hak Ja Han Moon being jealous of anyone, especially a schoolgirl like me. She had been only a year older than I when she married Sun Myung Moon.

At thirty-eight, pregnant with her thirteenth child, she still had the flawless skin and facial features of a great beauty.

She was outwardly generous to me, summoning me to her room that first week to give me a dress she no longer wore and a lovely gold chain. I took the chain off in her bathroom as I tried on the dress and mistakenly left it on the sink. She sent her maid to me later at Belvedere to give me the necklace. Mrs. Moon opened her closet and her purse to me, but from the very first, I felt she closed her heart.

The position of first daughter-in-law in a Korean family is, by tradition, an exalted one. She will inherit the role of mother and be the anchor of the family. There is even a special term for first daughter-in-law in Korean: *mat mea nue ri*. It was clear from the beginning that I would not fill this role in the Moon family. I was too young. "I had to raise Mother and now I have to raise my daughter-in-law, too," the Reverend Moon always said. It was only later that I recognized that no outsider would have been allowed a key role in the Moon family. As an in-law, one had to know one's place. For me that meant when the family was gathered, being the last person to sit in the seat farthest away from Sun Myung Moon.

Given the attention of customs officials that I had attracted at the airport, the Reverend Moon decided it would be prudent to stage a piano recital after all. I was in a panic. I had not practiced. I had brought no music with me. My mother assured me that I could get by with a Schumann piece I had memorized for class at Little Angels. I thought perhaps I remembered it well enough. Hyo Jin and Peter Kim, the Reverend Moon's personal assistant, drove me into New York City one afternoon to give me a chance to practice on the stage of Manhattan Center, the performing arts facility and recording studio owned by the church in midtown, where the recital would be held.

I sat alone in the backseat of one of the Reverend Moon's black Mercedes, staring out at the city as its skyscrapers came into view. I knew I should be impressed, but it was a cold, gray January day. My only impression was how lifeless New York City seemed. In retrospect, that dead feeling may have had more to do with my own emotions; they were as frozen as the concrete landscape outside my window.

At Manhattan Center, we met Hoon Sook Pak, the daughter of Bo Hi Pak, one of the highest-ranking officials in the church. She was Hyo Jin's age; he had lived with her family in Washington, D.C., during his tumultuous middle-school years. She would later become a ballerina with the Universal Ballet Company, Korea's first ballet troupe, founded by Sun Myung Moon. They greeted one another warmly in English, though both spoke fluent Korean. I stood there mute while they chatted at great length. I could feel my cheeks burn. Why were they ignoring me? Why were they being so rude? I got even angrier when Hyo Jin left me in a small anteroom while he went to talk to some other people. "Stay here," he instructed as if I were a puppy he was training to obey.

I felt a surge of that familiar stubborn pride that had provoked so many childhood arguments with my brother Jin. As soon as Hyo Jin was out of sight, I went exploring. The performing arts center is adjacent to the old New Yorker Hotel, now owned by Sun Myung Moon. The church uses the hotel to house members. The entire thirtieth floor is set aside for the True Family, to accommodate them on their overnight stays in New York City. I wandered around, jiggling the doorknobs of locked rooms.

Hyo Jin was furious when he returned to find that his pet had not stayed put, as ordered. "You can't just go off like that. You are in New York City. It's dangerous," he screamed. "Someone could have kidnapped you." I said nothing but I thought,

"Pooh! Who would kidnap me?" Mostly I hated that this rude boy thought he could tell me what to do.

Hundreds of church members filled the concert hall on the night of my performance. I was a small part of the evening's entertainment. I was the third of several pianists to play. I wore a long pink gown that my mother had bought for me before we left Korea. My stomach was doing somersaults, whether from the sushi I'd eaten at lunch or from the prospect of performing for the True Family, who were seated in the theater's VIP box. In Jin, Hyo Jin's sister, spooned out Pepto-Bismol for me to drink. It worked. I thought of that pink liquid as I did dog food: one of the wonders of America.

I played too quickly. The audience did not know I was done, so there was a delay in the applause. I was just relieved that I had made it through the piece and only missed a few notes. As soon as I got backstage, Hyo Jin and In Jin told me to change into my street clothes. I did as they said, not realizing there would be a curtain call for all the performers at the end of the evening. I could not go onstage dressed so casually, so I took no bows with the others.

In the Moons' suite in the New Yorker after the show, the Reverend Moon was so pleased with the evening that he decided that a real piano competition should be an annual event. Mrs. Moon, however, was icy toward me. "Why didn't you take your bow with the others?" she snapped. "Why did you change your clothes?" I was taken aback. What could I say? That I had done as her son instructed? Hyo Jin watched me squirm and said nothing. I just bowed my head and accepted my scolding.

My failure to appear for the curtain call was not my first infraction, it turned out. Mrs. Moon had been keeping track of my missteps. She enumerated them all for my mother the next day. I had been rude to enter their home wearing my boots; I had been careless to leave the necklace on the sink; I had been ungracious not to eat heartily at mealtime; I had been thoughtless not to take a bow at curtain call. In addition, she told my mother, Hyo Jin complained that my breath was stale. Mrs. Moon sent my mother to me with words of caution and a bottle of Listermint mouthwash.

I was devastated. If first impressions were the most lasting, my relationship with Mrs. Moon was doomed my first week in America.

The wedding was set for Saturday, January 7, in order to accommodate the school schedules of the Moon children. There was no marriage license. We had had no blood tests. I was a year below the legal age to marry in New York State. My Holy Wedding to Hyo Jin Moon was not legally binding. Not that I knew that, or cared. The Reverend Sun Myung Moon's authority was the only power that mattered.

We attended breakfast with the Reverend and Mrs. Moon in the morning. My mother urged me to eat. It would be a long day. There would be two ceremonies. A Western ritual would be held in the library of Belvedere. I would wear a long white dress and veil. Afterward there would be a traditional Korean wedding, for which Hyo Jin and I would wear the traditional wedding clothes of our native country. A banquet would follow in New York City.

My mother asked Mrs. Moon if I might have a hairdresser arrange my hair and apply my makeup. A waste of money, Mrs. Moon said; In Jin would help. I worshiped In Jin as a member of the True Family, but I was not so certain I trusted her to be my friend. She did as her parents asked, winning their praise for her kindness to me, but I could see that I was no more her type than I was Hyo Jin's. As she dusted my face with powder, she offered me some advice. I would have to change, and fast, if I was going to fit in with the Moon children, especially my husband. "I know Hyo Jin better than anyone," she told me. "He does not like quiet girls. He likes to have fun, to party. You need to be more outgoing if you want to make him happy."

Hyo Jin looked pleased enough when he stopped by to see me just before the ceremony, but I knew I was not the source of his happiness. On this day he would be his father's favorite, the good son, not the black sheep. He even agreed to trim his long shaggy hair to please his parents.

As I walked alone down the long hallway that led to the library and my future, an old Korean woman whispered to me, "Don't smile or your first child will be a girl." That was an easy instruction to follow, and not just because I knew the great disappointment that greeted the birth of females in my culture. My wedding day was supposed to be the happiest day of my life, but all I felt was numb. I want to weep for the girl I was when I look at the photographs in my wedding album. I look even more miserable in those pictures than I remember feeling.

There was a crush of people on both sides of me as I entered the library and made my way across the room to the Reverend and Mrs. Moon in their long white ceremonial robes. The library was very hot, packed with people, all of whom were strangers to me except for my parents. It was an impressive room, its dark wood-paneled walls lined with old, unread books, its high ceilings hung with chandeliers. It was hard not to believe in that setting that I was fulfilling God's plan for me and for the future of the True Family charged by him with establishing Heaven on earth. I was an instrument of his larger purpose. The marriage of Hyo Jin Moon and Nansook Hong was no silly, human love match. God and Sun Myung Moon, by uniting us, had ordained it.

It was a smaller group of family and church leaders who attended the Korean rites upstairs in Belvedere. I was learning that the Moons do the most momentous things in life in a hurry, so I barely had time to arrange my hair in the traditional style before I was summoned. I forgot to dot my cheeks in red in the customary manner, a failure noted by Mrs. Moon and the ladies who surround her. Hyo Jin and I stood before True Parents at an offering table laden with food and Korean wine. Fruits and vegetables were strewn beneath my skirt as part of a folk tradition meant to symbolize the bride's desire to produce many children.

I remember little of the actual ceremony. I was so tired that I relied on the flash of the official church photographer's camera to keep me focused. I was grateful for orders to "stand here" or to "say this." If I kept moving, I would not collapse.

A driver took Hyo Jin and me back to East Garden to change our clothes for the reception that would be held in the ballroom of Manhattan Center. He delivered us to a small stone house up the hill from the mansion. With its white porch and charming stone facade, it looked like something out of a fairy tale. This is where Hyo Jin and I would live. We called the place Cottage House. There was a living room, a guest room, and a small kitchen on the first floor. Upstairs was a small bathroom and two bedrooms. Our suitcases, I saw, had been delivered to the larger of the bedrooms.

Hyo Jin insisted that we have sex. I begged him to wait until the night — True Parents expected us to be ready to leave within the hour — but he would not be put off. I did not want to be naked in front of him. I slipped into bed to remove my clothes, a practice I would continue for the next fourteen years. I had read the books my mother gave me, but I was totally unprepared for the shock of sexual intercourse. When Hyo Jin got on top of me I did not know what to expect. He was very rough, excited at the prospect of deflowering a virgin. He told me what to do, where to touch. I just followed his directions. When he entered me, it was all I could do not to cry out from the pain. It did not take very long for him to finish, but for hours afterward, my insides burned with pain. "So this is what sex is," I kept thinking.

I began to cry, from pain, from exhaustion, from shame. I felt we were wrong not to wait. Hyo Jin kept trying to shush me. Didn't I enjoy it? he wanted to know. It was very "ouchy," I told him, using a little girl's word for a woman's pain. He said he'd never heard that reaction before, confirming all the rumors I had heard in Korea. Hyo Jin had had many lovers. I was shocked and hurt that he would confess his sin in such a callous and cavalier way. I wept even harder, until his sharp tone and angry rebuke forced me to dry my tears. At least I now knew what sex was and who my husband was. It was horrible; he was no better.

While we were dressing, a kitchen sister called to say that True Parents were waiting for us in the car. We rushed downstairs and into the front seat of a black limousine. Mrs. Moon looked at me accusingly. "What delayed you?" she snapped. "There are people waiting." Hyo Jin said nothing, but our flushed faces and hastily arranged clothing made our actions evident. I was glad the Moons were in the backseat so that they could not see my shame.

I fell asleep on the drive into Manhattan but my rest was short-lived. The ballroom of Manhattan Center was filled with banquet tables and hundreds of people, most of them American members. They cheered as we entered and took our seats at the head table. I was tired of all the hoopla, but there still were hours of entertainment and dining ahead of me. It was an American meal of steak and baked potatoes and ice cream and cake. My mother urged me to eat, but everything tasted like sand. Despite the Korean flavor of the entertainment, the entire evening was conducted in English. I understood not a word of the many speeches and toasts raised in honor of Hyo Jin and me. I smiled when the others smiled and applauded when the others did likewise.

The language barrier had the effect of making me a spectator at my own wedding. I was in this group but not part of it. I looked around at all the Moons singing, clapping. Everyone looked so happy. It was pretty exciting to watch. I was yanked out of my isolation when my father, who also did not understand English, told me he suspected I would be asked to make some brief remarks. "In English?" I asked, terrified. "No, no," my father reassured me. "Hyo Jin will translate for you." My father told me to keep it short, to thank God and the Reverend Moon and to promise to be a good wife to Hyo Jin. When the time came I did as my father said. The room erupted in shouts of "What did she say?" from the non-Korean audience. "Oh, it was nothing important," Hyo Jin told them as he went on to make his own remarks in English to tumultuous applause.

I kept my hands in my lap as I clapped. The Reverend Moon instructed me to lift them onto the table and told me to applaud more openly to demonstrate my joy on my wedding day and my appreciation of Hyo Jin. I did as he instructed, thinking all the while: "I am such an idiot. Can't I do anything right?"

The festivities did not end even after we returned to East Garden. It is a Korean tradition for wedding guests to strike the soles of the groom's feet with a stick for his symbolic thievery of his bride. Back at Cottage House, Hyo Jin put on several pairs of socks in preparation for this ritual assault. The Reverend and Mrs. Moon laughed as church leaders tied Hyo Jin's ankles together so he could not escape. Every time they hit Hyo Jin's feet Father would express mock outrage: "Stop, I will pay you not to hit my son." Those wielding the stick would take his money and resume their beating. "I'll give you more money if you stop," the Reverend Moon would shout and again the laughter would begin as they stuffed Father's money into their pockets and began hitting Hyo Jin again.

I watched the proceedings from a soft armchair that threatened to swallow me straight into sleep. Everyone commented on my calm demeanor. "She does not cry out to them to stop hitting her husband." I was not calm; I was numb. At the urging of the crowd, I tried to untie his ankles but I was so tired Hyo Jin had to do it himself.

The next morning we all gathered at the Reverend Moon's breakfast table. Hyo Jin disappeared early, I don't know to where. I stayed to wait on the Reverend and Mrs. Moon. I was not certain what my role should be in the True Family, and my new husband was little help in guiding me. I fell naturally into the role of handmaiden to Mrs. Moon.

It was not until after the wedding that anyone suggested to me that Hyo Jin and I might take a honeymoon. He wanted to go to Hawaii, but the Reverend Moon suggested Florida instead. Ours was not a conventional wedding trip. We made an odd threesome: husband, wife, and personal assistant to Sun Myung Moon. The Reverend Moon had handed his assistant, Peter Kim, five thousand dollars, with instructions to drive us to Florida. No one told me where we would be going or what we would be doing. My mother, accustomed to the formality of East Garden, packed a suitcase full of prim dresses for me, and I tossed in a single pair of blue jeans and a T-shirt.

Peter Kim and Hyo Jin sat in the front seat of the blue Mercedes. I sat alone in the back. They spoke in English for the eleven-hundred-mile trip down the East Coast. My sense of isolation was complete. The two men decided where and when we would stop to eat or sleep. I remember fighting off tears at a gas station rest room. I could not figure out how the hand dryer worked. I thought I had broken it when it would not stop blowing hot air. It was a small moment, but a lonely one. Such a simple thing and I had no one to ask for help.

I brightened a little when we arrived in Florida and Peter Kim suggested taking me to Disney World. I was a fifteen-year-old girl. I could not imagine a more wonderful vacation spot. Hyo Jin was unenthusiastic. He had been there many times before. He reluctantly agreed to stop in Orlando. It was cold. A light drizzle was falling, but I did not care. I walked down Main Street USA toward Cinderella's castle and understood exactly why they call Disney World the Magic Kingdom. I kept my eyes peeled for Mickey Mouse or any of the familiar costumed characters, but I would not have an opportunity to see any of them. Ten minutes after we arrived, Hyo Jin declared that he was bored and wanted to leave. I was astounded by his selfishness, but I followed a few steps behind as he led the way back to the Mercedes.

The Reverend Moon had suggested we drive to give me a chance to see some of the United States, but Hyo Jin soon ran out of patience with that plan as well. He summoned a security guard from East Garden to fly down to Florida to pick up the car. We were flying to Las Vegas, he told me.

I had no idea where or what Las Vegas was and neither Hyo Jin nor Peter Kim bothered to enlighten me. Neither did they tell me that the Reverend and Mrs. Moon and my own mother and father were vacationing there. I did not know we would be joining our parents until we walked across the hotel restaurant to the table where they were seated. My mother chastised me for gazing distractedly around the room as I walked toward them. It would only have been disrespectful, I told her, if I had known that the Moons were there and I did not!

I was all the more confused when I learned that Las Vegas is a gamblers' paradise. There were slot machines in the restaurants, casinos in the hotels. What were we all doing in a place like this? Gambling is strictly prohibited by the Unification Church. Betting of any kind is seen as a social ill that undermines the family and contributes to the moral decline of civilization. Why, then, was Hak Ja Han Moon, the Mother of the True Family, cradling a cup of coins and feverishly inserting them one after another into a slot machine? Why was Sun Myung Moon, the Lord of the Second Advent, the divine successor to the man who threw the money changers out of the temple, spending hours at the blackjack table?

I dared not ask, but I did not need to. The Reverend Moon was eager to explain our presence in a place I had been taught was a den of sin. As the Lord of the Second Advent, he said, it was his duty to mingle with sinners in order to save them. He had to understand their sin in order to dissuade them from it. I should notice, he said, that he did not sit and bet at the blackjack table himself. Peter Kim sat there for him and placed the bets as the Reverend Moon instructed from his position behind Peter Kim's shoulder. "So you see, I am not actually gambling, myself," he told me.

Even at age fifteen, even from the mouth of the Messiah, I recognized a rationalization when I heard one.

5

I returned to East Garden a married woman in the eyes of the Unification Church, but to all appearances, I was still a child in need of schooling. If I had harbored any doubts about my second-class status in the family of Sun Myung Moon, the discussions about my education certainly clarified my standing.

With the exception of my new husband, who at nineteen still had not completed high school, the school-age children of the Reverend Moon attended a private academy in Tarrytown. Mrs. Moon made it clear that she had no intention of paying the forty-five-hundred-dollar-a-year tuition at the Hackley School for me. Public school would do.

Early in February, Peter Kim drove me to Irvington High School to enroll me in the tenth grade. We stopped at a convenience store first to buy a notebook and some pencils. I would use the name Nansook Hong. No one was to know of my marriage or of my relationship with the Moon family. Peter Kim presented himself to the principal as my guardian. My report cards would be sent to him.

I had been in the top 10 percent of my class at Little Angels Art School back in Seoul, but the prospect of attending an American school filled me with dread. I walked behind Peter Kim through the noisy corridors of this typical suburban high school, taking in the laughter and casual dress of the teenagers rushing past me. How would I ever fit into this scene of pep rallies and junior proms? How would I even understand my English-speaking teachers? How would I ever reconcile being a serious student at school and a subservient wife at home? How would I be anything but lonely living this double life?

I woke every day by 6:00 A.M. in order to greet the Reverend and Mrs. Moon at their breakfast table. The mornings were crazy in the mansion kitchen. No one was ever certain what time the Reverend and Mrs. Moon would come downstairs, but when they did, they expected to be served immediately. The two cooks and three assistants would have prepared a main course, but as often as not, they would have to scurry if the Moons preferred something else. I would already have had a bite to eat in the kitchen before the Moons arrived at the table with a host of church leaders. I would drop to my knees for a full bow when they appeared and wait to be dismissed to the care of the driver who delivered me to school.

I was usually very tired in the morning because Hyo Jin never came home before midnight and demanded sex when he did. More often than not, he was drunk when he stumbled up the stairs of Cottage House, reeking of tequila and stale cigarettes. I would pretend to be asleep, hoping he would leave me alone, but he rarely did. I was there to serve his needs; my own did not matter.

I tiptoed around our room in the mornings, though there was little danger of waking my husband. He slept soundly well into the day; sometimes he was still sleeping when I returned from school. He would rouse himself, shower, and then return to Manhattan to make the rounds of his favorite nightclubs, lounges, and Korean bars. At nineteen, Hyo Jin had no trouble being served in the Korean-owned establishments he frequented. He often took his younger brother Heung Jin, then fifteen, and his sister In Jin, sixteen, with him on his late-night drinking jaunts.

Hyo Jin invited me to join them only once. We drove to a smoky Korean nightclub bar. It was obvious that the Moon children were regular customers; all the hostesses greeted them affectionately. A waitress brought Hyo Jin a bottle of Gold Tequila and a box of Marlboro Lights. In Jin and Heung Jin drank right along with him, while I sipped a glass of Coca-Cola.

I tried to hold them back, but the tears came in spite of my best efforts. What were we doing in a place like this? All of my childhood I had been taught that members of the Unification Church do not go to bars, that followers of Sun Myung Moon do not drink alcohol or use tobacco. How could I be sitting in this place with the True Children of the Reverend Moon while they engaged in the very behavior that Father traveled the globe denouncing?

In the world of funhouse mirrors I had entered, their behavior was not the problem. Mine was. "Why are you being like this?" Hyo Jin demanded before moving in disgust to another table. "You are spoiling everyone's good time. We came out to enjoy ourselves, not to be your baby-sitter." In Jin slipped into the chair beside me. "Stop crying or Hyo Jin will get very angry," she warned me sternly. "If you act like this, he won't like you." I had no time to compose myself before my husband yelled, "Let's go. We're taking her home."

No one spoke to me during the long drive to East Garden. I could feel their disdain pressing against me in the overheated car. "Don't cry," I kept telling myself. "You'll be home soon."

Just before Hyo Jin dropped me off, he picked up one of my classmates, a Blessed Child who shared the Moon siblings' passion for fun. She squeezed into the backseat, not even acknowledging my presence. They practically left skid marks on the driveway in their rush to return to New York.

That was the first of so many nights I cried myself to sleep. On my knees for hours beside our bed, I begged God to help me. "If you sent me here to do your will," I prayed, "please guide me." I believed in every chamber of my young heart that if I failed God in this life, I would be denied a place in Heaven with him in the next. What good is a happy earthly life if you don't go to God?

My knees were raw with carpet burns early the next morning when Mother summoned me to her room. Hyo Jin and the others still were not home. Where were they, she wanted to know. Why wasn't I with them? Prostrate before her on the floor, I wept as I recounted the events of the previous evening. It was a relief to share this awful burden with Mother. Maybe now something would change. Mrs. Moon was very angry, but not at Hyo Jin, as I had expected. She was furious with me. I was a stupid girl. Why did I think I had been brought to America? It was my mission to change Hyo Jin. I was failing God and Sun Myung Moon. It was up to me to make Hyo Jin want to stay home.

How could I tell her that when her son did stay home, things were no better? He had usurped the living room in Cottage House for the use of his rock 'n' roll group, the U Band. I hated their all-night practice sessions. The whole house shook when they played or listened to music on his stereo. Hyo Jin insisted that my training in classical music had made me a snob, but my distaste for his band had less to do with the music they played than with the way they behaved in our home. Band members would begin to assemble in the early evening, joined often by other Blessed Children who lived nearby. No sooner would I hear the guitars tuning up than the smell of marijuana smoke would drift upstairs, where I would be doing my homework.

My shock was a source of amusement to Hyo Jin and his friends, I knew, but the truth is my feelings about them were conflicted. I did not want to engage in proscribed behavior, but I was so very lonely upstairs with my schoolbooks. I did not want to join them, but I longed to be asked. I found myself living in an upside-down world, mocked by my peers for believing what we all had been taught, and chastised by my elders for failures that were not my own.

How could I tell Mrs. Moon that her children's barhopping was the least of their sins? I said nothing while she berated me. It was not long afterward that Mrs. Moon called my mother to her room to catalog my failings. In Jin had reported that I had worn my wedding ring to school. In Jin said I was asking around about Hyo Jin's old girlfriends.

I had done no such things, but it was impossible to defend myself before the Reverend and Mrs. Moon without seeming to criticize their own children, and that would not be tolerated. I tried to explain this to my own mother, but her only counsel was that I must be more careful not to offend the True Family. I must be cautious when I spoke. I must pray to become more worthy. That didn't seem possible. I was criticized at every turn, judged guilty without a fair hearing. Too often falsely accused, I became wary of trusting anyone.

How I wished that my father or my brother Jin would come from Korea! The Moons had sent my father back to Seoul soon after the wedding. Jin was still there, too, waiting to finish high school and obtain a visa to join his wife, Je Jin Moon, in the United States. When he came, I knew Jin would be preoccupied with his own life. He talked of attending college at Harvard, and the Reverend Moon seemed willing to send him, my brother's academic success a feather in the Messiah's cap. I was thrilled for Jin but sad for myself; I would have to remain in East Garden, surrounded by those who hated me.

Un Jin Moon was an exception. She was a year younger than I. She did not get along very well with In Jin either. We became friendly soon after my arrival at East Garden. I will always be grateful for Un Jin's kindness in those initial months. Everything was so new and I was so terrified of doing the wrong thing. At the first Sunday-morning Pledge Service I attended in East Garden, for example, I wore my long white church robes, only to discover all the Moons dressed in suits and dresses. I was mortified as only a teenager who is conspicuously dressed can be. I was embarrassed by my ignorance and hurt that no one had offered me guidance to such simple practices. Un Jin stepped in to fill that role, telling me what to expect at family gatherings and church ceremonies.

The Pledge Service was held in the study adjacent to the bedroom of the Reverend and Mrs. Moon. I was amazed at those services to realize that the Moon children did not know the words to the Pledge that I had been reciting from memory since I was seven years old. After the prayer service, the church sisters would bring snacks for the True Family: juice, cheesecake, doughnuts, and Danish. I would serve the Reverend and Mrs. Moon until it was time for us to go to Belvedere at 6:00 A.M., when the Reverend Moon preached his regular Sunday sermon before a gathering of local members.

It was an honor for me as a young woman to be able to hear Sun Myung Moon preach every week. He spoke in Korean, so it was easy for me to follow him. The American members relied on the rough translation provided by his assistants. I wish I could capture what it was about the Reverend Moon's sermons that touched my heart. It was not that he was especially profound, or particularly charismatic. In truth, he was neither. Mostly he urged us to dedicate our lives to serving God and humanity by becoming moral and just individuals. It was a noble calling. Most of us in that room at Belvedere on Sunday mornings really believed, however naively, that by our goodness alone we could change the world. There was an innocence and a gentleness about our beliefs that is seldom reflected in the denunciations of Unification Church members as cultists. We may have been seduced into a cult, but most of us were not cultists; we were idealists.

While the other Moon children went drinking in New York, Un Jin and I would stay up late into the night baking in the mansion's kitchen, chatting in Korean. Un Jin was a wonderful cook and a generous spirit, sharing her chocolate chip cheesecakes and homemade cookies with the security guards who had an office in the basement of the mansion.

The church members who composed the household staff were more accustomed to taking orders than gifts from the Moon children. The True Family treated the staff like indentured servants. The kitchen sisters and baby-sitters slept six to a room in the attic. They were given a small stipend but no real salary. The situation was little better for security guards, gardeners, and handymen who took care of the Moon properties. The Moons' attitude was that church members were privileged to live in such close proximity to the True Family. In exchange for that honor, they were ordered around by even the smallest of the Moons: "Bring me this." "Get me that." "Pick up my clothes." "Make my bed."

Sun Myung Moon taught his children that they were little princes and princesses and they acted accordingly. It was embarrassing to watch and amazing to see how accepting the staff were of the verbal abuse meted out by the Moon children. Like me, they believed the True Family was faultless. If any of the Moons had complaints with us, it must reflect not on their expectations but on our unworthiness. Given that mind-set, I was especially grateful for Un Jin's kindness. She never acted superior toward me; she seemed to like me for myself.

In Jin disapproved of my friendship with her sister but she could be nice to me herself when it suited her purpose. She came to me once, asking to borrow some clothes so she could sneak out that night. Her own room was next to her parents' suite in the mansion and she did not want to risk running into Father. Why not? I asked. She told me that recently she had come into her room on tiptoe about 4:00 A.M. It was still dark. She thought she was in the clear, when she saw Father's shadow in a chair across the room.

As Sun Myung Moon struck her over and over again, his daughter told me, he insisted he was hitting her out of love. It was not her first beating at Father's hands. She said she wished she had the courage to go to the police and have Sun Myung Moon arrested for child abuse. I lent her my best blue jeans and a white angora sweater and tried to hide how shocked I was by her story.

As much as anything about my new life in the True Family, the antipathy between the Moon children and their parents stunned me. Early on, I was disabused of the idea that this was a warm and loving family. If they had reached a state of spiritual perfection, it was often hard to detect in their daily interactions with one another. Even the smallest children were expected to gather for the 5:00 A.M. family Pledge Service on Sundays, for instance. The little ones were often sleepy and sometimes cranky. The women would spend the first few minutes trying to settle them down. The Reverend Moon would become enraged if our efforts to shush them did not succeed immediately. I remember recoiling the first of so many times that I saw Sun Myung Moon slap his children to silence them. Of course, his slaps only made them cry more.

Hyo Jin never disguised his contempt for Father and Mother. He seemed to consider them as little more than convenient sources of cash. We had no checking account or regular allowance when we were first married. Mother would just hand us money, a thousand dollars here, two thousand dollars there, on no particular schedule. On a child's birthday or a church holiday, Japanese and other church leaders would come to the compound with thousands of dollars in "donations" for the True Family. The cash went straight into the safe in Mrs. Moon's bedroom closet.

Later on, Mrs. Moon told me that fund-raisers in Japan had been assigned to provide money for the support of Hyo Jin's family and that funds would be sent regularly for that purpose. I had no idea how the mechanics of this worked. The money did not come directly to us. In the mid-1980s, money deposited in the True Family Trust was wired to Hyo Jin, and the other adult Moon children, every month. Hyo Jin received about seven thousand dollars a month, deposited directly into the joint checking account we had established at First Fidelity Bank in Tarrytown. The specific source of that money, beyond "Japan," was never clear to me.

Hyo Jin would go to Mother regularly for large sums of cash. She never said no, as far as I could tell. He stashed his money in the closet of our bedroom, dipping into his cash reserves whenever he headed out to the bars.

I was terrified one evening when he began screaming and throwing things around our room as he prepared for one of his evenings in Manhattan. "I'm going to kill you, you bitch," Hyo Jin yelled, as he rummaged through his closet, knocking clothes from their hangers and ties from their rack. "What did I do?" I asked apprehensively. "Not you, stupid. Mother. She's trying to ruin my life." His money was missing. He assumed Mother had come into Cottage House and taken it in order to curtail his drinking. I was doubtful. I had seen no evidence that either the Reverend Moon or Mrs. Moon tried to exercise any control over their children's wild behavior.

As I picked up his rumpled clothes, I found a wad of cash on the closet floor, wedged between a pair of shoes. It must have fallen out of a coat pocket. I counted more than six thousand dollars. Hyo Jin snatched the money from my hand, continuing to denounce Mother with a string of profanities as he nearly knocked the door from its hinges on his way out to the bars.

School, as difficult as it was for me, was a haven of sanity compared with the chaos of Cottage House. In English class I memorized lists of vocabulary words with no idea what they meant. In biology class I stared blankly as the teacher spoke directly to me and the class convulsed with laughter at my total lack of comprehension. It was only in math class that I saw a glimpse of the competent student I once was. For those forty minutes we all spoke the universal language of numbers. I was only a sophomore but I was enrolled in a twelfth-grade algebra class that covered material I had mastered in fourth grade in Korea.

I sat with other Blessed Children from Korea at lunch and sometimes studied with them as well. My position as the wife of Hyo Jin Moon lent a formality to our relationship that precluded real friendship. That cafeteria table was just one more place where I did not quite fit in. Two of my Korean classmates came to Cottage House one afternoon to study with me. They asked for a house tour. I showed them the practice room crammed with guitars and amplifiers and drums of the U Band. I showed them the bedroom and my study, where Mrs. Moon had installed a desk and bookcases for me.

"But where do you sleep?" one of the girls asked. "In the

bedroom, of course," I said, realizing too late that they were staring at the queen-sized bed. As members of the church, they knew of my marriage to Hyo Jin Moon, but they must have assumed it had not been consummated. That was not such a foolish assumption, I realize now. The age of consent in New York State is seventeen. Hyo Jin could have been arrested for statutory rape.

My embarrassment turned to shame when one of the Blessed Children turned on the television and an X-rated movie in the VCR came on the screen. I had never even seen Hyo Jin use the VCR. I checked the television cabinet and it was full of similar movies. Hyo Jin only laughed later when I confronted him about the pornographic films. He liked sexual variety, he said pointedly, in his life as well as in his entertainment. I should know that he could never be satisfied with one woman, especially a girl as prim and pious as I.

Hyo Jin even went to his mother to complain about my lack of sexual maturity. She called me to her one day to discuss my wifely duties. It was very awkward. I had trouble following her euphemisms about being a lady during the day and a woman at night. We must be friends to our husbands in the day but fulfill their fantasies at night, she said; otherwise they will stray. If a husband does stray, it reflects a wife's failure to satisfy him. I must try harder to be the kind of woman Hyo Jin wants. I was confused. Hadn't Sun Myung Moon chosen me for my innocence? Was I now expected to be a temptress? At fifteen?

I was beginning to see the truth: our marriage was a sham. Hyo Jin had gone through with the wedding, but he had every intention of living the life he had before. I suspected that Hyo Jin was having sex with the hostesses at the Korean bars he frequented, but I had no proof. When I would ask him what he did when he stayed out all night, he told me that it was impudent of me to question the son of the Messiah. I would lie awake in our bed, imagining that I heard his car, when it was only the sound of the wind.

Soon after our wedding, I had physical proof of his promiscuous lifestyle, but I was too naive to recognize it. Within weeks of our marriage, painful blisters began to appear in my genital area. I had no idea what had triggered the eruption of such terrible sores. Perhaps it was a normal reaction to sexual intercourse. Perhaps it was a nervous reaction.

It was no such thing, of course. Hyo Jin Moon had given me herpes. For years I would have to undergo laser treatments and apply topical ointments whenever the rash erupted. I spent one entire night soaking in a warm tub after a laser treatment inadvertently burned the delicate skin in the affected area. Hyo Jin watched me crying in agony in that tub that night and never told me the true source of my pain. It was years before my gynecologist told me explicitly that I suffered from a sexually transmitted disease. I needed to know, she said, because in the age of AIDS, Hyo Jin's adulterous behavior was not just a risk to his soul. It was a risk to my life.

In the spring of 1982, though, I knew only that Hyo Jin did not love me. Within weeks of our wedding, he told me we should go our separate ways before we ruined each other's lives. "We can't," I replied, stunned and tearful. "Father matched us. He says we must live together. We can't just split up." That was when Hyo Jin told me that he had protested my selection, that he had never wanted to be matched to me, that he went through with the wedding only to please his parents. He had a girlfriend in Korea, he said, and no plans to give her up.

I don't know which was more painful, his infidelity or the delight he took in flaunting it. Had he wanted to be discreet, Hyo Jin could have spoken to her privately. Instead he took sadistic pleasure in telephoning her in front of me from the living room in Cottage House. When he wanted to isolate me in East Garden, he spoke English to his friends and family. When he wanted to hurt me in my home, he spoke Korean to his girl-friend. "You know who I'm talking to, so go away," he would laugh, before loudly proclaiming his love for the girl at the other end of the telephone line.

Several weeks after our wedding, Hyo Jin left for Seoul with no word to me on why he was going or when he might return. He did not come home for months. He was not there the morning I suddenly became ill during a birthday celebration for one of his younger siblings. My mother helped me from the table, knowing instinctively what I did not even suspect. I was pregnant.

I responded to my pregnancy like the child I was. How would I finish high school? What would the other kids say? The larger questions, about my lack of preparedness for moth-erhood, about the perilous state of my marriage, were too diffi-cult for me to face. It was easier to worry whether I could make it through the school year without my condition's becoming apparent to my classmates.

The news of his impending fatherhood did not bring Hyo Jin rushing home from Seoul. He never even called or wrote to me. I called him once, only to have him chastise me for wasting Father's money. He hung up so abruptly that the Korean opera-tor had to tell me my call was disconnected. I felt as though I had been slapped. When he did call to talk about the preg-nancy, Hyo Jin spoke to Peter Kim, not to me. I was about to enter the kitchen one morning in the spring when I heard Peter Kim relaying to my mother the substance of that tele-phone call. I held my breath while I eavesdropped. What could possibly happen next? Even I was not prepared for what I overheard.

It was Hyo Jin's position that since we were not legally married, he was under no obligation to me, he had told Peter Kim. He intended to marry his girlfriend, who was not a member of the church. If the Reverend and Mrs. Moon wanted to take care of me and the baby, that was their choice. He wanted out. I was very scared, listening to Peter Kim and my mother, who said very little. Could Hyo Jin do this? What would happen to me and my baby? How could Hyo Jin break apart what Sun Myung Moon had joined together?

Hyo Jin soon returned from Korea and, without a word of apology or explanation to me, moved out of Cottage House. "I'm sure Father will take care of you and the baby," he said coldly. He even had the temerity to call to say that he would come by later that night to retrieve a prescription to treat his herpes. I was so incensed that before he arrived I unscrewed every light bulb in Cottage House so that he would have to stumble his way to the medicine chest. What satisfaction I took in my childish prank was short-lived. He was gone and I was alone and pregnant.

I had no idea where he was. It was not until later that I would learn that he had used the money we were given as wedding presents to pay for his "fiancée's" airfare to the United States and to rent an apartment for the two of them in Manhattan. On his return to East Garden from Korea, he had told the Reverend and Mrs. Moon that he intended to live with the woman he chose. Neither parent made any attempt to stop him. I always believed that the Moons were afraid of their son. Hyo Jin's temper was so volatile, his moods so irrational, that the Reverend and Mrs. Moon would go to any lengths to avoid a confrontation with him.

Instead, True Parents sent for me. I bowed before them, remaining on my knees, my eyes downcast. I hoped they would embrace me; I prayed they would reassure me. On the contrary, the Reverend Moon lashed out at me. I had never seen him so angry; his face was twisted and red with rage. How could I have let this happen? What had I done to so displease Hyo Jin? Why couldn't I make him happy? I did not lift my head for fear Sun Myung Moon would strike me. Mrs. Moon tried to calm him, but Father would not be appeased. I had failed as a wife. I had failed as a woman. It was my own fault Hyo Jin had left me. Why hadn't I told Hyo Jin that I would go with him?

My own thoughts made little sense. How could I go with him? To live with him and his girlfriend? I had high school to finish. I was frightened by the Reverend Moon's fury but I was also hurt at being wrongly accused. Why was it my fault that Hyo Jin had taken a lover? Why was I to blame because the Reverend Moon's son did not obey his father? I knew better than to voice these thoughts, but I had them just the same. It was my lot to humble myself before them, to take their abuse, and to speak only when spoken to. Tears burned my cheeks. I stayed on my knees, silent before the Lord of the Second Advent, but I seethed inside at the injustice of his attack on me. "Get out," he finally screamed, and I scrambled to my feet. I ran all the way back to Cottage House, blinded by my tears.

I felt utterly abandoned. My mother was no use to me. She was trapped in the same belief system that ensnared us all. If Sun Myung Moon was the Messiah, we must do his will. None of us was free to choose. It was my fate to be in this situation. I had to deal with it as best I could. Only God could help me. In my room at Cottage House, I wept and prayed aloud for God not to forsake me. If he could not ease my pain, I prayed he would make me strong enough to withstand it.

I was full of self-loathing for my weak tears. I was ashamed to cry in front of God. He had chosen me for this holy mission and I was not only failing him, I was surrendering to self-pity.

I prayed for God to strengthen my faith, to grant me the humility to accept the suffering he sent me.

On one such occasion, I had not realized that my mother was downstairs, listening to my prayers. When I came down, her eyes were as red as my own. It must have been hard for her to watch her daughter suffer so and feel powerless to help. I am only guessing at her emotions, though. We never spoke of our feelings. Perhaps we feared that if we acknowledged one another's pain, we would only be driven deeper into despair.

I was learning early in my marriage that hiding my feelings would be the key to self-preservation. I spent my days going through the routines of a seemingly carefree schoolgirl and my evenings on my knees in desperate prayer. Every afternoon that spring, I paced around the wide circular driveway in front of the mansion, trying to sort out my thoughts. One of Sun Myung Moon's early disciples joined me one day as I walked. No one in the Moon family had offered me any comfort. I was only assessed blame, which I was duty bound to accept. The church elder circled the pavement with me, urging me not to worry. My misery could harm my baby, he warned. Hyo Jin would come to his senses, he promised. I was embarrassed that my humiliation was such public knowledge, but I was grateful for the kindness of a respected elder.

That spring my brother Jin had finally come from Korea to join Je Jin at Belvedere. He had barely arrived when this crisis erupted: One afternoon the Reverend Moon summoned In Jin, Jin, and me to his room. "Should we throw Hyo Jin out of the family for what he has done?" the Reverend Moon asked us all, though it was clear that he expected only his daughter, In Jin, to answer. In Jin argued that Hyo Jin was young and wild but that he would listen to reason, that he would come home in his own time. It would be destructive for the church, as well as the

True Family, to disown the heir apparent to the Unification Church. Jin agreed. I said nothing.

If Hyo Jin returned, Father said, we must all forgive him and help him adjust to his responsibilities. I, especially, must hold no grudge, the Reverend Moon instructed. He conceded that this was a difficult time for me but said I owed it to the baby to pray for God to soften my heart toward my husband. He and Mrs. Moon would get Hyo Jin back. The rest of us were to welcome him warmly on his return.

The next morning Mrs. Moon took one of the prayer ladies with her to the Deli, a diner in Tarrytown. What I did not know was that Mother had arranged to meet Hyo Jin's lover there. She arrived defiant, intending to fight for my husband. She told Mrs. Moon they would not let religion stand in their way, that Hyo Jin was prepared to leave the Unification Church for her.

I was told it was a spirited performance. But his girlfriend left that diner with a full wallet and an airplane ticket to California. The Moons paid her off, sending her to Los Angeles in the care of a Korean woman whom she would soon ditch in order to make her own way in the world.

The Moons were very pleased with themselves. They had gotten Hyo Jin back home to East Garden. Never mind that they were ignoring the underlying issues that made him leave in the first place. Never mind that he was returning even angrier than when he had left. By all appearances, everything was back to normal, and appearances were everything to Sun Myung and Hak Ja Han Moon.

One morning soon after Hyo Jin's return, I came to greet True Parents at their breakfast table. I was surprised to see that they had been joined by the Buddha Lady, the Buddhist fortune-teller who had blessed my match to Hyo Jin the previous fall in Seoul. Mrs. Moon urged her to tell us what the future held for Hyo Jin and me. "Nansook is a winged white horse. Hyo Jin is a tiger. This is a good match," she said. "Nansook will have a difficult time in life but her fortune is very good. Hyo Jin's fortune is tied to hers. He can be great only if he sits on Nansook's back and together they fly."

Mrs. Moon was so pleased by the Buddha Lady's optimistic forecast that she went out and bought me a diamond-and-emerald ring — the fortune-teller had told her that green was my lucky color. A few days later the Buddha Lady came to see me secretly at Cottage House. "Please remember me when you are a very powerful woman," she said. "Remember the good fortune I saw ahead for you."

What lay ahead for me was nothing like what the Buddha Lady foresaw. Hyo Jin was furious that his parents had interfered in his love life, but he was also a realist. He was in no position to follow his lover to California. He had no money, no job, no high school diploma, no means of support besides his parents. In the end, Hyo Jin was all talk. True love paled next to the prospect of being cut off from Father's money.

Hyo Jin and this girlfriend would continue to correspond for years. He often left her love letters out in the open for me to find. When Hyo Jin learned that she had moved in with a new lover in Los Angeles in 1984, he was so distraught that he shaved his head.

In the spring of 1982, though, he had returned to Cottage House more angry than heartbroken. The indifference Hyo Jin had felt toward me in the winter had hardened into something much colder, much more frightening. I embodied his lack of choices in life. I represented his dependence on the two people he most needed and most despised in this world: his parents. Hyo Jin Moon would spend the rest of our life together punishing me for it.

6

I was pregnant with Sun Myung Moon's grandchild at the same time that he and Hak Ja Han Moon were expecting their thirteenth baby.

Mrs. Moon's obstetrician had warned her after the birth of their tenth child that another pregnancy could endanger her health, if not her life. The Reverend Moon simply had her change doctors. He was determined to bring as many sinless True Children of the Messiah into the world as possible.

However, the Moons were less committed to rearing those children. No sooner was a baby born to True Mother and True Father than it was assigned a church sister who acted as nanny and nursemaid. During my fourteen years in East Garden, I never saw the Reverend or Mrs. Moon wipe a nose or play a game with any of their children.

The Reverend Moon had a theological explanation for the kind of parental neglect he and Mrs. Moon exercised and that I had endured in my own childhood as the daughter of two of his original disciples: the Messiah came first. He expected believers to dedicate themselves to public proselytizing on his behalf; the pursuit of personal family happiness was a self-indulgence.

The Reverend Moon even designated particular couples among his original disciples to assume responsibility for the moral and spiritual development of each one of the Moon children. Assuming those parental duties himself, the Reverend Moon argued, would distract him from his larger mission: the conversion of the world to Unificationism.

Sun Myung Moon was not unaware of the bitterness this attitude engendered in his children. "My sons and daughters say that their parents think only of the Unification Church members, especially the 36 Couples," the Reverend Moon said in a speech in Seoul just months before my wedding. "I eat breakfast with the 36 Couples, even chasing my own sons and daughters away. The children naturally wonder, 'Why do our parents do this? Even when our parents meet us someplace, they don't really seem to care for us.'

"It is undeniable that I have loved our church members more than anybody else, neglecting even my wife and children. This is something Heaven knows. If we live this way, following this course in spite of our children's opposition and neglecting our family, eventually the nation and the world will come to understand. Our wives and children will understand, as well. This is the kind of path you have to follow."

Apparently the Reverend and Mrs. Moon had little idea of the real trouble that was brewing along that path. Soon after I enrolled at Irvington High School, In Jin and Heung Jin transferred there from Hackley. Father claimed he had abandoned the private school because his children were being tormented by teachers who mocked them as Moonies, but the truth was that some of the Moon children were terrible students. Once in public school, they adopted the dress and slang and behavior of their most wayward classmates. They even assumed Western names to use among their new friends. In Jin, for instance, called herself Christina for a while, and then Tatiana. When Hyo Jin joined them for parties, he called himself Steve Han.

It wasn't only through their assumed names that the older Moon children sought to distance themselves from the True Family. Most took a perverse pleasure in ignoring every tenet of their religion. The Moons paid scant attention. They had more public problems to contend with that spring: Father was about to stand trial for being a tax cheat.

The previous fall, only weeks before Hyo Jin and I were matched, an indictment had been handed up against Sun Myung Moon in federal court in New York. He was charged with filing false personal tax returns for three years, failing to report about $112,000 in interest earned on $1.6 million in bank deposits, and failing to disclose the acquisition of $70,000 worth of stock. An aide was charged with perjury, conspiracy, and obstruction of justice for lying and fabricating documents to cover up the Reverend Moon's crime.

The Reverend Moon returned to the United States from a trip to Korea to plead not guilty to those charges. Father told twenty-five hundred cheering supporters on the steps of the federal courthouse in New York that he was a victim of religious persecution and racial bigotry: "I would not be standing here today if my skin were white and my religion were Presbyterian. I am here today only because my skin is yellow and my religion is the Unification Church."

Father had made similar pronouncements earlier that year when a jury in Great Britain concluded at the end of a six-month libel trial that a national newspaper, the *Daily Mail,* had been truthful in describing the Unification Church as a cult that brainwashed young people and broke up families.

The High Court jury described the church as a "political organization" and urged the government to consider rescinding its tax-exempt status as a charity. The jury also ordered the Unification Church to pay $1.6 million in court costs at the end of the trial, the longest and costliest in British history.

In the New York tax case, Father had been released on a personal recognizance bond of $250,000, cosigned by the Unification Church and one of its umbrella corporations, One Up Enterprises. The trial began April 1. Despite the advanced stage of her pregnancy, Mrs. Moon accompanied Father to federal court every day. Un Jin and I went only once. I did not understand a single word of the proceedings because of the language barrier, but I did not need to understand what was being said to know what was happening in that courthouse. Sun Myung Moon was being persecuted, not prosecuted.

Father had explained to us that what was happening to him was part of a long history of religious bigotry in the United States. Even though early settlers came to North America seeking religious freedom, they had found intolerance instead. In his Sunday-morning sermons at Belvedere, he told us of innocent women who had been tried and hanged as witches in Massachusetts, of Quakers who were stoned in the South, of Mormons who were murdered in the West. The Internal Revenue Service investigation that resulted in Father's trial was part of that shameful tradition.

Every morning there would be a pilgrimage of family and staff to Holy Rock, a clearing in the woods on the eighteen-acre East Garden estate. Father had blessed as sacred ground this spot high on a hill above the Hudson River. It was a beautiful, unspoiled place. Praying there I felt closer to God and further from the twentieth century than in any other place I had ever seen. It was a place for quiet contemplation, looking little different in 1982 than it did when Henry Hudson first explored this area of the continent in 1609.

Father prayed at Holy Rock alone before dawn every day. The prayer ladies, older women including my mother, held vigils there every day of the six-week trial. Sometimes the True Children and Blessed Children from the surrounding area would meet there to pray for Father's exoneration. I remember how cold it was on that hill. I was pregnant and my joints would ache from the chill, but my discomfort was small next to the suffering Father was enduring.

There were tears when Father was convicted in May, but I'm not sure that anyone, outside the inner circle of the Reverend Moon and his advisers, understood the gravity of his situation. None of us really believed that U.S. District Court judge Gerard Goettel would do what was in his power and sentence Father to fourteen years in prison. The gloom in East Garden about Father's conviction for tax fraud had been offset by the ruling of a separate court in New York that the Unification Church was a genuine religious organization and entitled to tax-exempt status.

Two months later, Judge Goettel sentenced the Reverend Moon to serve eighteen months in prison and pay a twenty-five-thousand-dollar fine. Father accepted the sentence stoically. In the Reverend Moon's scheme of things, his imprisonment — his martyrdom — was providential. Mose Durst, president of the Unification Church of America, even compared Father's conviction to that of Jesus Christ "for treason against the state." The Reverend Moon's lawyers filed an immediate appeal. "We have the utmost faith that through the court system in America, justice will be done and our spiritual leader fully vindicated," Mose Durst told the press. "As with all of the world's great religious leaders, he has been met with hatred, bigotry and misunderstanding."

In response to threats by prosecutors to have the Reverend Moon deported, the church hired Harvard Law School professor Laurence Tribe, an expert on constitutional law, to handle his appeal. Professor Tribe argued successfully that deporting Father would deprive him of contact with his six American-born children, who then ranged in age from two months to ten years. Judge Goettel agreed that deportation would be "an excessive penalty," though he acknowledged that the public animosity toward the Reverend Moon made this "a difficult decision, one that is bound to be unpopular with a lot of people." Father was allowed to remain at home, pending the outcome of his appeal.

Father seemed unfazed by his conviction. That summer, when Hyo Jin was in Korea again, I accompanied the Reverend and Mrs. Moon to Gloucester, Massachusetts, where the church owned fleets of fishing boats and a processing plant. The Reverend Moon has said he founded the so-called Ocean Church to feed the world's hungry. We all suspected he bought the fleets because he likes to go fishing. In Gloucester, Father owns Morning Garden, a mansion he purchased from the Catholic Church. (All of the Moons' residences had names designed to evoke the Garden of Eden: there was East Garden; Morning Garden; North Garden, in Alaska, where Father also owned a fishing fleet and two giant fish processing plants in Kodiak and a third in Bristol Bay; West Garden in Los Angeles; South Garden in South America; and yet another enormous estate in Hawaii.)

That summer, Father also rented a house in Provincetown on the tip of Cape Cod so he could fish even more. It was my responsibility to wait on Mother and the children on the beach while the kitchen sisters who accompanied us prepared meals. I would serve the family lunch on the beach, dry off the children after swimming, and generally act as Mrs. Moon's lady-in-waiting. It was a frustrating and thankless job. I could not swim unless she swam. I could not take a walk unless she did. I could not even visit the bathroom unless I was accompanying her. I was there to wait on her, no more, no less. At night I slept in a sleeping bag surrounded by her children, her cooks, and her maids. She boasted that she was providing us all with a relaxing vacation, but she and the children were the only ones who looked relaxed to me.

Despite my own pregnancy, I felt like a servant child in the Moon household. In East Garden, when the Moons were in residence, I was required to rise before they did and wait outside their bedroom for them to awaken. It was my duty as their daughter-in-law to serve the Moons their meals and to attend to Mrs. Moon's needs throughout the day. When I was not at school and on the weekends, I was at Mrs. Moon's side from morning until night. I spent most of this time waiting to be called upon to fetch her something, to serve her something, or to accompany her somewhere. I spent hours watching videotapes with her of the mindless Korean soap operas she enjoyed and I abhorred. I had to pay attention, though, in case she commented on the plot.

I ate my meals in the kitchen with the other children, while True Parents dined with church leaders and visiting dignitaries. We learned of developments in the tax case through whispers; Father never spoke with us directly about his situation. We were only children in his eyes.

I can't say that I disagreed. The kitchen was the one place in the compound that felt like a real home, with the little ones spilling their milk and the older ones chatting about school. I often fed Yeon Jin in her high chair. Hyung Jin was just a toddler. I would take him from the big round table in the kitchen out onto the hills of East Garden, where we would pick wildflowers. I grew up with the Moon children, more a sibling than a sister-in-law.

I would go with Un Jin sometimes to New Hope Farm, the horse farm that the Reverend Moon had purchased in Port Jervis, New York. An accomplished equestrian, Un Jin loved horses. The South Korean Olympic equestrian team trained there. Thanks in large measure to Sun Myung Moon's money, Un Jin would become a member of that Olympic team in 1988.

Heung Jin was the only other older Moon child who showed me much kindness my first year in East Garden. He was just a few months younger than I. He was a sweet boy. He kept a cat in his room. When she had kittens he could not bear to part with any of them, so they took over his room. Sometimes we would find Heung Jin sleeping in the small telephone alcove next to his bedroom because the cats had made it impossible for him to slip into his own bed. My first winter at East Garden, he had given me roses on my birthday, a gesture especially memorable because Hyo Jin did not even buy me a card.

I went to language school that summer and fall, trying to master English and disguise my advancing pregnancy from my older, mostly Spanish-speaking, classmates. Mrs. Moon had sent my mother back to Korea that summer to look after my younger siblings, so I found myself lonelier than ever in East Garden. My pregnancy was a more frightening than joyous adventure. I was plagued with debilitating morning sickness that I was too young to know would pass. I worried there was something terribly wrong with me or with my baby.

Hyo Jin was rarely at home. Whenever he got bored, which was frequently, he would announce that he was going to Korea for a "seven-day course" or a "twenty-one-day course," church training programs designed to bring one closer to God. Despite his announced intentions, word usually filtered back from Seoul that Hyo Jin was spending his time with bar girls or his old girlfriends. When he was at East Garden, he demanded sex every night, despite my protests that it was terribly painful.

More upsetting than the pain was the disgust he expressed as my waist and hips expanded with our growing child. For me, it was a miracle. For him, it was an affront. He called me fat and ugly. He made me cover my tummy when we had sex so that he did not have to see.

The Reverend Moon would say that I needed to pray harder for Hyo Jin to come back to God, that soon fatherhood would change him. Not incidentally, he said we must all pray for the health of the baby I was carrying. No one spoke of it above a whisper, but I knew that everyone in East Garden feared the baby might suffer the consequences of Hyo Jin's insatiable appetite for drugs and booze and unprotected sex.

I went to Lamaze childbirth classes alone. A driver would drop me off with my two pillows at Phelps Hospital. Every other pregnant woman was there with an attentive partner. The teacher paired me with a nurse who was studying the Lamaze breathing and exercise techniques. I felt that God had sent her to help me. Grateful as I was, my heart ached looking at all the loving couples, preparing for the birth of their babies. The women chatted about crib styles and car seats. They debated the merits of cloth versus disposable diapers. The men looked awkward but proud, placing their palms gently on their wives' bellies to feel the babies move inside. Hyo Jin had just scoffed when I asked if he would like to try. I spoke to no one for six weeks of classes. I wondered what they thought of me. I was alone and so much younger than all of them. I must have looked pitiable. I had to accept during those classes the truth that I pushed from my thoughts each night: Hyo Jin did not care about me or our baby.

My mother returned to East Garden in January in anticipation of the birth, which we expected in early February. She slept downstairs in Cottage House. It was good she was there because on February 27, when I began to have contractions, my husband wasn't. I was three weeks overdue. Hyo Jin had returned from Korea, but despite the impending birth, he went to New York every night to the bars. That's where he was when I went into labor. My mom walked me around the house to ease my discomfort, but at 10:00 P.M. we finally called the doctor, who told us it was time. Hyo Jin had not bothered to leave a telephone number where we might reach him, so an East Garden security guard drove me and my mother to the hospital.

I was terrified. Even on the fifteen-minute drive from East Garden to Phelps Hospital, the pain intensified. I could not believe what was happening to my body. I had not missed one childbirth class; I had read up on labor and delivery; but nothing prepared me for the searing pain that ripped across my belly with each contraction. I could not sit comfortably in the car. I felt every pothole or turn in the road like a knife in my womb.

My mother stayed with me during that long, sleepless night. She held my hand and dried my tears when the pain came. Every hour I would beg the nurses to check to see if I had dilated enough to deliver this baby. One centimeter. Two centimeters. My cervix opened as slowly as the hands of the clock turned. I thought the night would never end. I thought my skin would split open. I thought I would die.

Hyo Jin did not come to the hospital all night. When he did come in the morning, he looked hungover and did not stay long. He watched the waves of pain pass over me as each contraction crested. He saw me cry. He heard me moan. Then he fainted. It was quite a sight, this man who thought he was so tough splayed out on the labor room floor. The nurses laughed as they helped Hyo Jin to his feet. If I had been in less agony, I might have seen the humor. Instead I saw only that once again he would leave me alone when I needed him.

In the waiting room, Mrs. Moon huddled with the prayer ladies and fortune-tellers. They sent word to the labor room that the baby must be born before noon in order to achieve the best future. The doctor was willing to help. "If that's your culture, I'll do what I can," she said. My mom had to wait outside the delivery room, so I depended on the compassion of the nurses to pull me through. They were wonderful, although I confess wanting to strangle them when they laughed at my impotent pushes. The baby's head would emerge and then retreat. I just didn't have the strength. The doctor performed an episiotomy and used forceps to ease the baby out of the birth canal.

It was a girl. She had a mass of black hair. She had red marks on her face from the pressure of the forceps. Her eyes were closed. I felt sorry for her. She was so small and fragile looking — just under seven pounds — that I was afraid to hold her. I could feel the nurses' disapproval. They exchanged glances when I did not take the baby right away. I worried that they thought I didn't love my daughter. Nothing could have been further from the truth. I was just so young and so scared.

In the waiting room, news that the baby was a girl was greeted with the disappointment I had expected. It was my duty to produce a grandson and again I had failed the Moons. The reaction would have been the same in Korea, even had I not been a member of the Unification Church. Boys are still valued more highly than girls in my culture. But my responsibility to produce a son was tied to the future of the Unification Church. As the eldest son of True Father and True Mother, Hyo Jin Moon would inherit the mission of the church. It was my duty to deliver the son who would follow Hyo Jin as the head of the church.

I was overwhelmed by feelings of incompetence after the birth of Shin June. She could not latch on to my nipple and the nurse and I could not figure out how to help her. The nurses on the maternity ward were impatient with my youth and my difficulties with English. But I knew then what women mean by maternal instinct. I had never seen anything as miraculous as my baby's tiny fingers. I had never felt anything as soft as her translucent skin. I had never heard a more reassuring sound than her gentle breathing. Even though I did not know what to do, I looked at my baby and felt a love I had never known before. We would figure it all out together, God, my baby, and I.

The baby and I were discharged from the hospital at 1:30 P.M. on March 3. Hyo Jin drove us home to East Garden in Father's car. The Reverend Moon was waiting at home to bless the new baby. He prayed, pointedly I thought, that God would work to restore Hyo Jin through the baby's birth. But there was to be no miraculous change in Hyo Jin's behavior. He stayed with us on our first night home from the hospital. After that, though, it was back to the bar scene.

My mom remained at East Garden for several months to help with the baby. I felt guilty for needing her as much as I did. The ease with which she cared for Shin June only underscored my own fumbling manner. I would have been lost without my mother, but it pained me to leave her awake all night with the baby while I slept. As much as I loved my baby, maybe because I loved her so much, this was one of the loneliest periods of my life.

I began to keep a diary after my daughter was born. To read it now is to weep for the girl I once was. The diary itself is testament to my youth — the cover is a portrait of Snoopy, the canine cartoon character.

March 6, 1983: "Hyo Jin came home at 2:00 A.M. last night and slept through until two o'clock in the afternoon. Then he went out with Jin Kun Kim."

Eight days after a baby's birth in the Unification Church, a ceremony of dedication is performed. The number eight signifies a new beginning in Unificationist numerology. The ceremony is not a baptism, since we believe that Blessed Children are born without original sin on their souls. The dedication is more of a prayer service to thank God for the birth of the new child.

On March 7 we held such a ceremony for Shin June. My diary records the event: "Hyo Jin was holding the baby. Father prayed. We passed the baby among us. Everyone kissed her cheeks. During breakfast, Mother was holding her the whole time. She was in a good mood. She said the baby looked just as Hyo Jin did when he was born. Father said her eyes were like those of a mystical bird and that this meant she would be witty. Westerners have round eyes that show what they are thinking. Easterners' eyes are dark pools that can't be penetrated. Father said this means we have a bigger, deeper heart."

The next evening, only five days after Shin June and I came home from the hospital, Hyo Jin left for Korea. He did not have to go; I think he wanted to get away from us, from the responsibility that the baby and I represented. "I try to think that I am less sad than other times, since the baby is with me. But after I put her to sleep and came to my room, I was overcome with loneliness. It seems like there is a big hole in my heart and I am very sad and empty," I wrote in my diary. "I pray to God for Hyo Jin's safe arrival in Korea. I thank God for giving me my baby so I can fill this lonely, empty, and sad heart. Tears keep pouring down."

I wanted so much for Hyo Jin to share my joy at the birth of our precious daughter, but I knew we were not in his thoughts once he arrived in Korea. "I wonder if Hyo Jin arrived safely in Korea. Even though I asked him to give me a call when he arrives, I don't expect it," I wrote in my diary. "I am going to

I am singing at a Moon family birthday celebration at the mansion in East Garden. The Reverend Sun Myung Moon would make each of us sing at family and church gatherings, a practice I dreaded because of the poor quality of my voice.

I am flanked here by my mother, Gil Ja Yoo Hong, on the left, and an assistant to Mrs. Moon, Malsuk Lee. Our placards protest the incarceration of the Reverend Sun Myung Moon in Danbury Federal Penitentiary for tax evasion.

The Moon family gathers for a typical birthday celebration for one of Sun Myung Moon's children. The fruit is piled high on the offering table in front of us. I am in the back row, second from the right. Hyo Jin is in the same row at the very end.

Hyo Jin and I and our four children in November 1990, at our suite at the New Yorker Hotel in Manhattan. We are dressed in the religious robes of the Unification Church. Ordinary members wear white robes. The robes of the family of Sun Myung Moon are decorated with gold braid.

Hyo Jin Moon and I celebrate his birthday with one of our daughters.

Six months before I fled the Moon compound, I posed with True Mother and True Father on the 100th Day anniversary of Shin Hoon's birth. Because his drinking and drug use left Hyo Jin in no condition to participate, we went without the traditional 100th Day celebration.

Hyo Jin Moon hauls an octopus aboard True Father's fishing boat off Kodiak, Alaska, where Sun Myung Moon maintains one of his many homes. From left to right: Sun Myung Moon, Hak Ja Han Moon, me (holding our son Shin Gil), and Hyo Jin.

One of my daughters greets Sun Myung Moon on his return from a trip overseas. The men applauding in the background are church members and leaders.

Celebrating Shin Gil's fifth birthday in February 1993. The Reverend Moon and Mrs. Moon did not know that I had had an abortion only days before this picture was taken.

In the family room at East Garden, I instruct my son Shin Gil how to bow before his grandmother, Hak Ja Han Moon. She is surrounded by grandchildren.

I am holding our first baby, and Hyo Jin is holding the youngest child of Sun Myung Moon.

I am holding my first baby, on the day of my high school graduation from Masters, a private school in Dobbs Ferry, New York.

On the day he was released from Danbury prison, Sun Myung Moon was surrounded by his wife and children. The banner hanging from the fireplace celebrates the birthday of Young Jin, one of his sons.

I am standing outside the mansion at East Garden with my first baby.

wait several days and then I am going to call him. I decided I am going to capture many beautiful pictures of the baby and send some to Hyo Jin."

It was not easy to capture those photographs in the early weeks. Like most babies, Shin June had trouble establishing a regular sleep schedule. She would cry all night and sleep all day. My mom was exhausted and I was wracked with guilt. "My mom raised her children and now she is raising her grandchild. I feel guilty to make her suffer like this. I really don't know much. I feel guilty toward my baby and I thank my mom," I wrote. "I gave her a bath. I washed her hair and put her in the bathtub. I couldn't even wash her with soap and my mom finished her bath. I thanked my mom and I felt ashamed. I feel bad and guilty toward my little girl. I feel very inadequate as a mother. I want to be a good mother but there are so many things that I don't know. I cannot stop feeling guilty toward her."

Days went by and still Hyo Jin did not call and still I waited. "I wonder what Hyo Jin is doing now. I wonder if he is thinking about his daughter even a little bit," I wrote. "Father asked, 'Did Hyo Jin call?' I felt bad since I had to answer no. I heard that Hyo Jin gave a talk to leaders about the wife's role. I wonder what he's doing right now."

I was not feeling well physically after the birth. Korean women take extra care to protect themselves after a baby's birth. We wrap ourselves in several layers of clothes to ward off the cold. No number of layers could keep away the chill I felt. I had never been sickly, but I was small. My body was not ready to give birth. I had pains in my joints that would worsen with each pregnancy. That March my emotional, physical, and spiritual miseries were in competition with one another. "My eyes are hurting all day long. My teeth are sensitive, so that I can't eat anything. I don't know why I don't feel well. I have a headache and my heart is heavy. I have to breast-feed the baby a little later. I feel bad toward her," I wrote. "I wonder what Hyo Jin is doing. He doesn't call. I don't even think about it, but I am still waiting for his call.

"It has been a long time since I prayed with all my heart. I became lazy after the baby was born. When I was pregnant, I was more conscientious and diligent in praying for the sake of the baby. But after the birth, I think I became inattentive. When I am down and disheartened, when I think of Hyo Jin, I look at the baby. Then my heart is filled with hope. She is all my hope. My only hope lies in her and I pray that Hyo Jin will come back. Once again, I thank God with all my heart for giving me my daughter. Amen."

March 18, 1983: "It's been raining hard since morning. The wind is also very strong. I've been sitting in front of my desk and loneliness fills my heart. I feel that I am all alone in this world. I often feel that there is nobody with me and I am removed from everybody. Even though my baby is in the next room, I feel like I am all alone. . . ."

March 19, 1983: "I had bad dreams yesterday and the day before yesterday. In the dream, Hyo Jin was with two other women even though he was married to me. I don't even want to think about it, but the dreams were very real. They are so vivid that it seems as if they are not dreams, but real. I can remember the women's faces so clearly. I have never seen them before. Last year when Hyo Jin brought his girlfriend to New York City and didn't come home for a week, I dreamed twice that he was with her. I knew her, but I don't know the women that I dreamed about this time. There were two different women on both days. Anyway, it is not a good dream. I don't know why I am dreaming this kind of dream. Maybe I am thinking about him too much! Or maybe this is Satan's test! I have no appetite and I think I am getting weak spiritually.

Before I gave the baby a bath, I called Hyo Jin. I don't under-stand why it is so difficult for him to call me. When I am alone or try to sleep, I can't stop thinking things about him. I try not to think but the thread of thought continues. I don't know why I am like this. I am afraid to be alone."

March 22, 1983: "Mom scolded me because I didn't eat breakfast because I have no appetite. I lost my appetite since having those bad dreams. Mom told me that if I become physi-cally weak Satan will invade, so I should eat, thinking I am bit-ing Satan! I heard Hyo Jin is doing well at the workshop but I still have bad dreams. Maybe Satan is testing me. I think I have become mentally and physically weak. I shouldn't lose to Satan. I should quickly get stronger physically and fulfill my responsibility to God, Hyo Jin, and our daughter."

March 27, 1983: "The rain and wind are very powerful. In spite of the bad weather and her tiredness, my mom went to Holy Rock for an hour at three o'clock. My poor mom and dad. I feel that they are not well and always suffering because of their daughter, because of me. I wonder whether Hyo Jin is doing well in the workshop, and what he is doing. I heard from my mom that on the sixth day he called his two girlfriends for an hour each! Satan invaded on the sixth day. Our Heavenly Father, how he is watching Hyo Jin and is worried. Our poor God."

March 31, 1983: "I was angry for no reason yesterday. Maybe it is Satan's test. I couldn't control myself. Since the birth of the baby, I cannot fit into my old clothes. I have been somewhat worried about that these days. I told myself, I shouldn't be doing this. I am seventeen years old now. I should be doing things and going places, but I have a baby and I have become a middle-aged lady. What a pathetic girl I am! I even regret being here. Why am I like this? Heavenly Father does not feel happy and I feel repentant. Yet I still feel that it is better to meet an ordinary man and receive his entire love. I know I shouldn't think like this. I repent, Heavenly Father!!"

April 4, 1983: "Monday, 2:00 A.M. When I write in the diary, I think about what I did today. Well, how did I spend the day? During the day, I try to forget about my situation, but while I write in the diary I organize my thoughts. I always feel empty inside. Is it because of him? While waiting to feed the baby when she wakes up, I read the letter that I found. It's a letter from the woman in L.A. Previously, I ripped up old letters that I have found from his other girlfriends. I don't know why I didn't tear up the new letter. I don't have any feelings about the letters. I am not even angry. I think about this as a pathetic situation. I wonder how I became like this. I am not upset at the women he is dating. I feel pity for them. The person I am upset with is Hyo Jin."

Hyo Jin did not return to East Garden until summer. Our daughter, a tiny newborn when he left, was by then a bright-eyed babbling baby. He seemed just as indifferent to her as he was when he went to Korea. I was at a loss, fearful for our future. That summer the Moons decided I could not return to Irvington High School. They worried that public school officials could get too curious about the cause of my extended leave of absence, that there would be rumors about the baby. I was still below the age of consent in New York when she was conceived. They did not need their son accused of child abuse or even rape.

I was admitted to the Masters School, a private school for girls in Dobbs Ferry, New York. I was very excited. I had been yearning to go back to school since spring. In my diary in April, I had written: "I should study very soon. I also have to practice piano. I am just wasting my time, not doing anything. I have to make plans to study." School would be a distraction from my loveless marriage and my depression. It would make me a better mother. I was full of hope for the first time since coming to East Garden.

One morning the Moons called me to their room. I was alarmed. When they sent for me, it usually meant I had done something wrong in their eyes. I never knew which one of them would be angry at me. Both of them had horrible, raging tempers, but they rarely were angry at the same time. This time it was Mrs. Moon who began shouting as soon as I fell to my knees to bow to them.

Did I know how much the tuition was at the Masters School? Did I have any idea how much money it would take to educate me? Why should they be burdened with this expense? I was not their daughter. They already had to pay to feed and clothe and house me. How much more did I want? She could barely speak, she was so furious. The Reverend Moon said nothing while she ranted. I kept my head bowed, bit my lip, and began to cry. I thought I had done everything the Moons wanted. I married their wayward son. I stood by him even when he left me, pregnant, for his girlfriend. I had given them a beautiful granddaughter. Why was Mother screaming at me?

Mrs. Moon said that Bo Hi Pak's daughter had received her high school diploma through a correspondence course. I could do the same. What did I need with a fancy education? I could do what Hoon Sook Pak had done. She was a ballerina now. It had all worked out. I could study at home and care for the baby at the same time.

I was stunned. My parents had always valued education. They sacrificed their own comfort to ensure that their seven children had the best schooling available. The Moons were going to let me get a diploma through the mail? I knew that I needed to go back to school, to see people my own age, to get out of the Moon compound for part of my day. I was so grateful when the Reverend Moon finally spoke up. Those correspondence courses are no good, he told Mother quietly; we have to send Nansook to school.

The two of them discussed the options as if I were not there, on my knees sobbing before them. They made every important decision about my life and then blamed me for the repercussions. I tried to will my tears to stop. I had done nothing wrong. I should not be crying. I could not help myself, though. When she had fully vented her rage, Mrs. Moon suddenly remembered I was still there. "Get out!" she shouted. I scrambled to my feet and tried to avert my eyes from the staff as I rushed down the stairs and back to Cottage House.

The entire summer went by with no mention of my education. One day in September, I was simply told that I would begin the eleventh grade the next day at Masters School. I was driven to and from school that year. In my senior year, I learned to drive. Hyo Jin had offered to teach me, but after one session of his screaming abuse, I told him I preferred to learn from one of the security guards at East Garden. It was the first time I had stood up to Hyo Jin. I knew I was not going to learn if he shouted, and he would not stop shouting. I even learned to parallel park, without ever leaving the Moon property.

I loved the Masters School. The academics were challenging and the student body included several Korean girls. Most of them were musicians, studying at Juilliard at Lincoln Center in New York City on the weekends. To them I was just another teenage Korean expatriate being educated in the United States. My parents, like theirs, were at home in Korea. None knew about my relationship with Sun Myung Moon. None knew I was a wife and a mother. They thought I lived with a guardian in Irvington. No one asked for more information than that, and I found myself grateful for the discretion of my Korean culture.

One girl at Masters School was especially sweet. She was younger than I and treated me like a big sister. When she needed a confidante, I was happy to fill that role. She could not bear to speak to her mother when her family telephoned from Seoul. Just the sound of her mother's voice would make her weep with homesickness.

I felt so sorry for her, but I envied her, too. It only occurred to me in comforting her that I did not experience the normal range of emotions of a girl my age. If I missed my mother or my family, I felt I was failing God. If I longed to go home, I felt I was resisting my fate. If I hated my husband, I felt I was doubting the wisdom of Sun Myung Moon.

I was free to feel my failure and my loneliness, but I was not free to express them. As a result, my friendships with classmates were strictly superficial, one-way propositions. I could not confide in anyone that school year when I realized I had suffered a miscarriage.

I had known for weeks that I was pregnant but had missed my first doctor's appointment. When I began to notice small amounts of blood staining my panties, I did not think much of it. When an ultrasound confirmed that I had lost the baby, I was devastated. I had to be hospitalized overnight for a D and C. Hyo Jin did not come to see me until it was all over. He found me weeping in my hospital room. Instead of comforting me, he said my tears disgusted him. He cared less that we had lost our baby than that I was making a scene. "You are very unattractive when you cry," he said, before leaving me alone with my loss.

I wished, then, that I had a real friend, but I knew that my life and the lives of the girls I sat alongside in the schoolroom were alike only on the surface. If I was going to survive in the True Family, I realized after Hyo Jin's heartless response to my miscarriage, I would need to compartmentalize my emotions even more than I had already done.

More than most young women my age, I was suspended between childhood and adulthood, with a foot in both worlds. I was still young and dependent enough that spring to ask my mother to pick out the long white dress I would wear to my high school graduation. I was also old enough to have a toddler at home, watching me get ready for the ceremony, where then–Vice President George Bush would give the commencement address at the request of his godchild, one of my classmates.

"Can I come, Mommy?" my daughter wanted to know. I longed to have my little girl with me on my big day, but I left her at home in East Garden. I had not figured out how to integrate the two very different worlds in which I lived.

7

December 22, 1983, dawned cold and damp in the Hudson River valley. The gloomy weather reflected the mood at East Garden. Father and Mother had left days before for a major speaking tour in Korea. The Reverend Moon was scheduled to address a rally in Chonju, South Korea, an antigovernment stronghold. There were fears for his safety because of his close ties to the repressive military regime of Chun Doo Hwan.

He had to go into the camp of the enemy, Father told us, because only by direct confrontation could he defeat the Communists, Satan's emissaries on earth. We thought Sun Myung Moon was the bravest man in the world. The prayer ladies spent the day at Holy Rock, praying for a successful and peaceful trip.

The link between religion and politics had been explicit for Sun Myung Moon since his childhood in Japanese-occupied Korea. The division of our country into Communist and democratic zones had further defined the lines of political demarcation for his religious ministry. The Communists had imprisoned him as an itinerant preacher. They had outlawed religious pluralism. They were the enemy. He devoted his public life to the spread of Unificationism and the defeat of Communism. For Sun Myung Moon one goal was inseparable from the other.

If Hyo Jin was concerned about his parents, there was no change in his behavior to indicate it. Early that evening he went into New York to visit the bars. I was at home alone with the baby when the telephone rang after midnight. It was one of the security guards. "There's been an accident," he said. I feared immediately for True Parents. "No, it's not Father," he said. "It's Heung Jin."

Heung Jin?

The second son of the Reverend and Mrs. Moon had been driving home from a night out with two Blessed Children when his car slammed into a disabled truck on an icy road not far from the Unification Theological Seminary in Barrytown, New York. Heung Jin and his friends often went to the seminary to use the firing range that the Reverend Moon's sons, all avid hunters, had built on the grounds. All three boys were hospitalized.

My brother, Peter Kim, and I rushed directly to the emergency room at St. Francis Hospital in Poughkeepsie, New York. None of us was prepared for what we found. Jin Bok Lee and Jin Gil Lee were injured, but not seriously. However, Heung Jin had suffered severe head trauma in the crash. He was in the operating room undergoing brain surgery when we arrived.

I watched Peter Kim walk to the pay phone in the corridor to call Father and Mother in Korea. He was weeping. "Forgive me. I am so unworthy," he began. "You left me in charge of your family and the most terrible thing has happened." The call did not last long. The Reverend and Mrs. Moon said they would be on the next plane home.

I had never been exposed to serious illness or life-threatening injury before. It was terrifying to see a boy my own age, especially a boy as sweet as Heung Jin, lying in an intensive care unit, attached to all manner of tubes and machines. He was unconscious. He lay perfectly still, the only sound the hum of the respirator that pumped oxygen into his inert body. We did not need a doctor to tell us the gravity of his condition.

We all went to New York to meet True Parents at the airport the next day. I'll never forget the stricken look on Mrs. Moon's ashen face. It was clear she had not slept since receiving Peter Kim's call. We followed the Moons to the hospital, where church members had all but taken over the ICU waiting room and were conducting a prayer vigil for Heung Jin.

The Reverend Moon concentrated on comforting everyone else before he entered Heung Jin's room. Mrs. Moon wanted only to be with her son. There would be no miracle. Heung Jin was brain dead. On January 2, 1984, the Moons made what must have been the hardest decision of their lives. With all of us gathered around his hospital bed, the ventilator that kept seventeen-year-old Heung Jin Moon alive was turned off. He died without ever regaining consciousness. Mrs. Moon clung to her son's lifeless body, her tears staining the crisp white bed linens. The Reverend Moon stood dry-eyed beside her, trying to console a mother who was beyond consolation.

The rest of us wept copious tears at the death of our brother, but the Reverend Moon ordered us not to cry for Heung Jin; he had gone to the spirit world to join God. We would be reunited with him one day. We all remarked with admiration on Father's strength, on his ability to put his love of God before the loss of his son. As a new mother, I was more mystified than impressed by Sun Myung Moon's reaction.

There was an enormous funeral for Heung Jin at Belvedere. At Mrs. Moon's instruction, the women and girls in the family wore white dresses; the men wore white ties with their black suits. Church members wore their white church robes. Upstairs as we got ready for the service, I felt my usual awkwardness. I was not a True Child, just an in-law, so I did not know quite where I belonged. I found my place at the edge of the family. The kitchen sisters had prepared all of Heung Jin's favorite foods to remind us of the boy we had lost. The table looked as if it had been laid out for a teenager's birthday party: hamburgers, pizza, and Coca-Cola.

I had never been to a funeral before. Heung Jin's open coffin was placed in the living room. It was a large room, but overflowing with two hundred people, it soon grew very hot. For three hours, friends and family offered testimonials to Heung Jin, to his goodness and his kindness. I wept openly, despite my promise to Father not to cry. I was not alone. The Reverend Moon instructed all members of the True Family to kiss Heung Jin good-bye. The littlest ones understandably were frightened. I lifted some of the smallest to kiss Heung Jin's cheek, as I did myself. He was so terribly cold.

Father walked to the front of the room and instantly all sounds of weeping ceased. He told the funeral gathering that Heung Jin was now the leader of the spirit world. His death had been a sacrificial one. Satan was attacking the Reverend Moon for his anti-Communist crusade by claiming the life of his second son. Like Abel before him, Heung Jin had been the good son. Hyo Jin looked wounded by Father's comparison, but he knew himself that he bore more of a resemblance to the Biblical Cain.

Heung Jin, Father said, was already teaching those in the spirit world the *Divine Principle*. Jesus himself was so impressed by Heung Jin that he had stepped down from his position and proclaimed the son of Sun Myung Moon the King of Heaven. Father explained that Heung Jin's status was that of a regent. He would sit on the throne of Heaven until the arrival of the Messiah, Sun Myung Moon.

I was stunned by the instant deification of this teenage boy. I knew Heung Jin was a True Child, the son of the Lord of the Second Advent, so I was ready to believe that he had a special place in Heaven. But displacing Jesus? The boy I had helped search for a lost kitten in the attic of the mansion at East Garden, he was the King of Heaven? It was too much, even for a true believer like myself. I looked around me, though, and the assembled relatives and guests were nodding gravely at this imparted revelation. I was ashamed of my skepticism but powerless to deny it.

Heung Jin's coffin was carried out to the hearse and driven to JFK International Airport for the long flight to Korea. The Reverend and Mrs. Moon did not accompany their son's body. Je Jin and Hyo Jin went home with their brother. Heung Jin was buried in a Moon family plot in a cemetery an hour outside of Seoul.

Almost immediately, videotapes began arriving at East Garden from around the world. Unification Church members in various states of entrancement were pronouncing themselves the medium through which Heung Jin spoke from the spirit world. It was so strange to watch these tapes. We would gather with Father and Mother around the television and watch one stranger after another purport to speak for Heung Jin. None of them offered any profound religious insights. None displayed any confirming familiarity with Heung Jin's life in East Garden. But all praised True Parents and reinforced Father's revelation that Jesus had bowed down to Heung Jin in Heaven.

I not only did not believe the claims in these tapes, I was offended that so many people would try to exploit the grief of the True Family in such a transparent attempt to gain favor with Father. I was naive. This was exactly the approach most likely to win Sun Myung Moon's affection. Father clearly was thrilled by this "possession" phenomenon, occurring spontaneously around the globe. It was impossible for me to tell whether the Reverend Moon actually believed his son was speaking through these people or if he was using their scam for his own purposes.

One theological problem with the deification of Heung Jin Moon was that Sun Myung Moon teaches that the Kingdom of Heaven is attainable only by married couples, not by single individuals. Father dealt with that expeditiously. Less than two months after Heung Jin died, a wedding ceremony was held in which Sun Myung Moon joined his dead son in marriage to Hoon Sook Pak, the daughter of Bo Hi Pak, one of his original disciples. Hoon Sook's brother, Jin Sung Pak, was married on the same day to In Jin Moon. The joint wedding on February 20, 1984, can only be described as bizarre.

In Jin was furious that Father had matched her to Jin Sung, a boy she could not stand. In Jin had many boyfriends; marriage was the last thing on her mind. She called Jin Sung "fish eyes," after the most distinctive physical characteristic of the Pak family. The truth was she had a crush on a younger boy. The year before, In Jin and I had shared a room in a Washington, D.C., hotel, where we were attending a Unification Church conference. She thought I was sleeping late one night when she telephoned this boy at his family's Virginia home. She was whispering softly and giggling in a girlish way that was unlike her in my experience. I realized she was flirting with him, telling him that even though Blessed Children were not supposed to kiss, she thought they could make an exception.

It was a dangerous infatuation. What neither of them knew at the time was that they shared the same father. The boy is Sun Myung Moon's illegitimate son. My mother had told me so a year before, but it was clear to me that night that no one had told them. That the boy had been born of an affair between the Reverend Moon and a church member was an open secret among the thirty-six Blessed Couples. It was not a romantic liaison, my mother had explained to me. It was a "providential" union, ordained by God, but one that the secular world would not understand. To avoid any misunderstanding, the baby was placed at birth with the family of one of Sun Myung Moon's most trusted advisers and was raised as his son. His real mother lived nearby in Virginia and played the role of family friend in his young life. The Reverend Moon has never acknowledged his paternity publicly, but by the late 1980s, the boy and the second generation of Moons were told the truth.

The placement of a baby in the home of an unrelated church member was not an isolated occurrence. It happened all the time. Infertile couples in the church simply were given a baby by members who had several children. Since we all belonged to the family of man and the only True Parents are the Reverend and Mrs. Moon, what difference did it make who actually reared a child? The Unification Church often dispensed with such legal niceties as adoption proceedings and simply shared out children in much the way one neighbor might lend another an extra garden hose.

We had gathered at the Belvedere mansion for the double wedding that February just as we had for my own two years before. In their white ceremonial robes, the Reverend and Mrs. Moon presided first over the wedding of their daughter In Jin to Jin Sung Pak. Immediately following the ceremony, the crowd fell silent as Hoon Sook entered the ornate library in a formal white wedding gown and veil. A beautiful young woman, she was twenty-one, an aspiring ballerina. The Reverend Moon would found the Universal Ballet Company in Korea to highlight her talent under the stage name Julia Moon.

She carried a framed portrait of Heung Jin down the aisle to Mother and Father. My husband, Hyo Jin, stood in for his dead brother next to the bride. He repeated the vows that Heung Jin was not able to recite. Hoon Sook was such a beautiful bride, I felt sorry that she would never be able to marry a living groom. But as my eyes moved from her to Hyo Jin, I felt something else stirring in me; it was envy. How much better, I thought, to be loved by a dead man than to live in misery with a man you do not love and who does not love you.

This ceremony would have seemed strange, indeed, to anyone outside the Unification Church, but the Reverend Moon frequently joined the living with the dead in matrimony. Older, single members were often matched to members who had gone to the spirit world. In what must stand as his ultimate act of arrogance, Sun Myung Moon actually had matched Jesus to an elderly Korean woman. Because the Unification Church teaches that only married couples can enter the Kingdom of Heaven, Jesus himself needed the intervention of the Reverend Moon to move through those gates.

A few years after their Holy Wedding, Julia Moon and the long-dead Heung Jin Moon would become parents. She did not actually give birth, of course. Heung Jin's younger brother Hyun Jin and his wife simply gave Julia their newborn son, Shin Chul, to raise as her own.

The civil authorities were unaware of these allegedly miraculous doings, however. Four months after Heung Jin's death, the U.S. Supreme Court, without comment, refused to review the Reverend Moon's conviction for federal tax evasion. Sixteen amici curiae briefs filed by organizations such as the National Council of Churches, the American Civil Liberties Union, and the Southern Christian Leadership Conference portrayed the case as one of religious persecution with profound implications for the free exercise of religion. If Sun Myung Moon could be targeted, the thinking went, what unpopular evangelist might be next?

"The precedent has been set for the government to examine the internal finances of any religious organization," warned the Reverend George Marshall of the Unitarian-Universalist Association.

The Reverend Mr. Marshall was one of four hundred religious leaders around the nation who spoke up in support of Moon in rallies staged across the country. The Reverend Edward Sileven, a Baptist minister from Louisville, Nebraska, compared Moon's plight to his own. The Reverend Mr. Sileven had served eight months in jail for refusing to obey a court order to close down his unaccredited fundamentalist Christian school. "People ask me, 'Don't you feel funny coming to a rally for the Reverend Moon?' But I'd rather fight for your freedom once in a while than come together with you all in a concentration camp."

Jeremiah S. Gutman, president of the New York Civil Liberties Union, organized an ad hoc committee of religious and civil rights leaders to protest what he called "an indefensible intrusion in private religious affairs."

A U.S. Senate Judiciary Committee panel chaired by Senator Orrin G. Hatch reviewed the Moon case and agreed.

We accused a newcomer to our shores of criminal and intentional wrongdoing for conduct commonly engaged in by a large percentage of our own religious leaders, namely, the holding of church funds in bank accounts in their own names. Catholic priests do it. Baptist ministers do it, and so did Sun Myung Moon.

No matter how we view it, it remains a fact that we charged a non–English speaking alien with criminal tax evasion on the first tax returns he filed in this country. It appears that we didn't give him a fair chance to understand our laws. We didn't seek a civil penalty as an initial

*means of redress. We didn't give him the benefit of the
doubt. Rather we took a novel theory of tax liability of less
than $10,000 and turned it into a guilty verdict and 18
months in federal prison.*

*I do feel strongly, after my subcommittee has carefully
and objectively reviewed this case from both sides, that
injustice rather than justice has been served. The Moon
case sends a strong signal that if one's views are unpopular
enough, this country will find a way not to tolerate, but to
convict.*

The Reverend Charles V. Bergstrom of the Lutheran Council
in America testified before Senator Hatch's committee, but he
was more subdued in his assessment of the Reverend Moon's
tax case. "I have a question about whether he had a fair trial.
The court denied Reverend Moon's request to have a judge
decide the case, and the judge told the jury not to consider him
a religious person for the purpose of the trial. But I also have to
ask: Why did he have to handle all that money?"

The answer was clear enough to anyone inside the church:
the Unification Church was a cash operation. I watched Japanese church leaders arrive at regular intervals at East Garden
with paper bags full of money, which the Reverend Moon
would either pocket or distribute to the heads of various
church-owned business enterprises at his breakfast table. The
Japanese had no trouble bringing the cash into the United
States; they would tell customs agents that they were in America to gamble at Atlantic City.

In addition, many businesses run by the church were cash
operations, including several Japanese restaurants in New York
City. I saw deliveries of cash from church headquarters that
went directly into the wall safe in Mrs. Moon's closet. From
here, on any given day, she might distribute five thousand dol-

lars to the kitchen staff for food or five hundred dollars to a child who had just won a game of hopscotch.

There was no question inside the church that the Reverend Moon used his religious tax exemption as a tool for financial gain in the business world. The pursuit of profit was central to his religious philosophy. A capitalist at heart, the Reverend Moon preaches that he cannot unify the world's religions without building a network of businesses to support believers. To that end, he has built or bought food processing plants, fishing fleets, automobile assembly lines, newspapers, companies that produce everything from machine tools to computer software.

No matter what the lawyers said in court, no one internally disputed that the Reverend Moon comingled church and business funds. No one had any problem with it. How often had I heard church advisers discuss funneling church funds into his business enterprises and political causes because his religious, business, and political goals are the same: world dominance for the Unification Church. It was U.S. tax laws that were wrong, not Sun Myung Moon. Man's law was secondary to the Messiah's mission.

The Reverend Moon's philosophy sounded benign enough: "The world is fast becoming one global village. The survival and prosperity of all are dependent on a spirit of cooperation. The human race must recognize itself as one family of man." What his civil libertarian allies outside the Unification Church failed to realize was that Sun Myung Moon, and only Sun Myung Moon, was the head of that family.

Using church funds to finance his anti-Communist political agenda was a given, part of the Unification Church philosophy. In 1980 the Reverend Moon had established CAUSA, an anti-Communist front that the church described as a "non-profit, non-sectarian, educational and social organization which presents a God-affirming perspective of ethics and morality as a basis for free societies." In practical terms that meant CAUSA supplied crucial funds to oppose Communist movements in El Salvador and Nicaragua.

The Reverend Moon was never shy about drawing attention to the roots of his anti-Communist beliefs. "The need for unity among the God-affirming peoples of the worlds became profoundly clear to the Reverend Moon when he was imprisoned and tortured for his Christian faith by North Korean Communists in the late 1940s. CAUSA is an outgrowth of his commitment to America and to world freedom."

In the 1980s Latin America was the focus of the Reverend Moon's anti-Communist zeal. The missionaries he sent to support anti-Communist sympathizers in the region did not come wearing church robes. They came in business suits, under the auspices of the many "scholarly" organizations that Father quietly established and funded without any overt reference to Sun Myung Moon or the Unification Church. With titles such as the Association for the Unity of Latin America, the International Conference on Unity in the Sciences, the Professors World Peace Academy, the Washington Institute for Values in Public Policy, the American Leadership Conference, and the International Security Council, the Reverend Moon's missionary arms had an academic veneer. Speakers to conferences sponsored by these groups, many of them prominent figures in the media, politics, and scholarship, rarely knew that their fees, hotel rooms, and meals were being paid for by Sun Myung Moon.

Personally, the Moons had an almost physical aversion to paying taxes. Lawyers for the church spent most of their time trying to figure out how to avoid them. That's why the True Family Trust fund was based not in a U.S. bank but in an account in Liechtenstein.

It is only in retrospect that I see the hypocrisy of Sun Myung Moon's claiming religious persecution for his efforts to manipulate the law for his own gain. At the time, I was an impressionable teenager, a new mother, a faithful follower. That year, I returned to Korea for the first time in order to secure a more permanent visa. I had been in the United States illegally for three years before the Moons decided it was time to legitimize my immigration status. I was not alone. East Garden was full of maids, kitchen sisters, baby-sitters, and gardeners who had come into the United States on tourist visas and just melted into the subculture of the Unification Church.

I had not really understood then that we were breaking the law. It would not have mattered to me. God's law supersedes civil law and Father was God's representative on earth. Even the importance of the Reverend Moon's trial the year before had escaped me. But prison? That I understood. We all were heartsick that Father would actually be locked up for a year and a half.

At 11:00 P.M. on July 20, 1984, Sun Myung Moon took up residence at the medium-security federal prison in Danbury, Connecticut. The day before surrendering to prison authorities, Father had met at the mansion in East Garden with church leaders from 120 countries. He assured them that he would simply move his base of operations from home to prison. His living accommodations would be quite different in Danbury, where he was housed in a dormitory-style building with forty or fifty other inmates. He was assigned to mop floors and clean tables in the prison cafeteria.

He was allowed visitors every other day. I dutifully accompanied Mrs. Moon in order to serve them both. I fetched food from the vending machines, slipping black extract of ginseng into cups of instant soup at Mother's instruction to give Father extra strength during his ordeal. The leaders of his various business enterprises and church leaders came to consult with him frequently. The business of the Unification Church continued uninterrupted.

Whenever we visited Father, he would give the children homework assignments, to write a poem or an essay. We would then read them to him on a return trip. I remember one he gave me, "The Life of a Lady."

In Jin took on the role of public defender of her father. In a rally for religious freedom in Boston, she told 350 supporters that Sun Myung Moon's plight was similar to that of Soviet dissident Andrei Sakharov, the Nobel Prize—winning physicist. "This is a very difficult time for me to bear and understand," she told the crowd. "In 1971 he came to this country obedient to the voice of God. For the last twelve years he has shed his tears and sweat for America. He told me God needs America to save the world. Now he is sixty-four years old and guilty of no crime. When I visited him in prison and saw him in his prison clothes, I cried and cried. He told me not to weep or be angry. He told me and millions of others who follow him to turn our anger and grief into powerful action to make this country truly free again."

In Jin shared the stage that night with former U.S. senator Eugene McCarthy, who denounced Father's incarceration as a threat to liberty. The Reverend Moon's prison term was turning into a public relations coup for the Unification Church. Overnight he went from being a despised cult leader to being the symbol of religious persecution. Well-meaning civil libertarians made Sun Myung Moon a martyr to their cause. They, too, were being duped.

Shaw Divinity School in Raleigh, North Carolina, awarded an honorary Doctor of Divinity degree to Father while he was imprisoned. The school cited Sun Myung Moon for his "humanitarian contributions in several areas: social justice, efforts to relieve human suffering, religious freedom and the fight against world communism." Joseph Page, the vice president of the school, insisted that the Unification Church's thirty-thousand-dollar contribution to Shaw Divinity School had "absolutely not" influenced the board of trustees to honor the Reverend Moon.

While he was in prison, the Reverend Moon sent Hyo Jin to Korea to direct a special workshop for Blessed Children, the sons and daughters of original members. "Previously, each was heading in his own direction, and there was no discipline among them," Sun Myung Moon would say later in a speech. "But now they have been brought together in a certain order. It is significant that this happened while I was serving my prison sentence because after Jesus' crucifixion, all his disciples separated and ran away. Now, during my incarceration, the Blessed Children from around the world came together, to the central point, instead of running away."

Even as Father was gaining respectability among mainstream Christians and consolidating his hold on the second generation of Unificationists during his time in prison, his son was growing in stature after death. Reports of messages from Heung Jin were proliferating, although some of them were less than profound: "Dear Brothers and Sisters of the Bay Area: Hi! This is the team of Heung-Jin Nim and Jesus here. We need to establish a foothold among you and bring true sunshine here to California," read one written on official Unification Church stationery. It was purportedly transcribed by a church member while in a trancelike state.

"Our brother has received messages from Heung Jin Nim, St. Francis, St. Paul, Jesus, Mary and other spirits have come to him as well," Young Whi Kim, a church theologian, wrote of one such medium. "They all refer to Heung Jin Nim as the new Christ. They also call him the Youth-King of Heaven. He is the

King of Heaven in the spirit world. Jesus is working with him and always accompanies him. Jesus himself says that Heung Jin Nim is the new Christ. He is the center of the spirit world now. This means he is in a higher position than Jesus."

Back on earth, after thirteen months in prison, the Reverend Moon was freed on August 20, 1985. He was released to the cheers of his new friends in the religious community. Both the Reverend Jerry Falwell of the Moral Majority and the Reverend Joseph Lowery of the Southern Christian Leadership Conference called on President Ronald Reagan to grant Father a full pardon. Two thousand clergymen, including Falwell, Lowery, and other well-known religious leaders, held a "God and Freedom Banquet" in his honor in Washington, D.C.

At East Garden it was as though Father had returned from a world speaking tour and not from a prison term. The old rhythms returned. The meetings around his breakfast table resumed. But something was different. There was a perceptible shift in the Reverend Moon's Sunday-morning sermons at Belvedere after his release from the penitentiary. He talked less and less about God and more and more about himself. He seemed obsessed with his vision of himself as some kind of historical figure, not merely as an emissary of God. Where once I had listened intently to his sermons in search of spiritual insight, I now found myself more uneasy and less engaged.

The Reverend Moon's hubris culminated later that year in a secret ceremony in which he actually crowned himself and Hak Ja Han Moon as Emperor and Empress of the Universe. Preparations for the lavish, clandestine event at Belvedere took months and hundreds of thousands of dollars.

Church women were assigned to research the regal robes of the five-hundred-year Yi dynasty that ended in the nineteenth century. Others were ordered to design solid-gold-and-jade crowns modeled on the ones worn by tribal kings. My mother was in charge of buying yards and yards of silk and satin and brocade material and finding seamstresses in Korea to turn these expensive raw materials into the costumes of a royal court. All twelve of Sun Myung Moon's children, all of his in-laws, all of his grandchildren, were to be outfitted as princes and princesses.

In the end Sun Myung Moon's crowning ceremony looked less like a historical reconstruction than like a popular Korean television soap opera set during the Yi dynasty. I felt silly, as though I were dressed for a period comedy rather than a sacred religious service. The Reverend Moon was aware enough of how an act of such monumental egotism would be received by the world that he banned photographs from being taken at the actual ceremony. Invited guests, all high-level church officials, who arrived with cameras had them confiscated by security guards, who blocked the entrances to gate-crashers.

In his gold crown and elaborate robes, Sun Myung Moon looked to me for all the world like a modern-day Charlemagne. The difference was that this emperor bowed to no pope. Since there was no authority higher than the Reverend Moon, the Messiah had to crown himself Emperor of the Universe.

The coronation was a turning point for me and my parents. For the first time we voiced our doubts to one another about Sun Myung Moon. It was not an easy thing to do. Much has been written about the coercion and brainwashing that takes place in the Unification Church. What I experienced was conditioning. You are isolated among like-minded people. You are bombarded with messages elevating obedience above critical thinking. Your belief system is reinforced at every turn. You become invested in those beliefs the longer you are associated with the church. After ten years, after twenty years, who would want to admit, even to herself, that her beliefs were built on sand?

I didn't, surely. I was part of the inner circle. I had seen enough kindness in the Reverend Moon to excuse his blatant lapses — his toleration of his son's behavior, his hitting his children, his verbal abuse of me. Not to excuse him was to open my whole life up to question. Not just my life. My parents had spent thirty years pushing aside their own doubts. My father tolerated the arbitrary way in which Sun Myung Moon ran his businesses, inserting unqualified friends and relatives into positions of authority, promoting those who curried favor and firing those who displayed any independence. My father survived at the top of Il Hwa pharmaceuticals by accepting the Reverend Moon's frequent public humiliations. For his part, the Reverend Moon left my father in place because Il Hwa continued to make money for him.

If the deification of Heung Jin and the crowning ceremony tested my faith, the emergence of the Black Heung Jin nearly destroyed it. Many of the reports of possession by Sun Myung Moon's dead son came from Africa. In 1987 the Reverend Chung Hwan Kwak went to investigate reports that Heung Jin had taken over the body of a Zimbabwean man and was speaking through him. The Reverend Kwak returned to East Garden professing certainty that the possession was real. We all gathered around the dinner table to hear his impressions.

The Zimbabwean was older than Heung Jin, so he could not be the reincarnated son of Sun Myung Moon. In addition, the Unification Church rejects the theory of reincarnation. Instead, the African presented himself to the Reverend Kwak as the physical embodiment of Heung Jin's spirit. The Reverend Kwak had asked him what it was like to enter the spirit world. The Black Heung Jin said that upon entering the Kingdom of Heaven, he immediately became all-knowing. The True Family need not study on earth because they were already perfected. Knowledge would be theirs when they entered the spirit world.

That rationale appealed to Hyo Jin as much as it offended me. He had flirted with some courses at Pace University and at the Unification Church seminary in Barrytown, New York, but my husband was more interested in drinking than in learning. I was put off by the suggestion that we did not have to work to earn God's favor. We in the Unification Church might be God's chosen people, but I believed our efforts on earth would determine our place in the afterlife. We had to earn our place in Heaven.

The Reverend Moon was thrilled with the news from Africa. The Unification Church had been concentrating its recruitment efforts in Latin America and Africa. Clearly a Black Heung Jin could not hurt the cause. Without even meeting the man who claimed to be possessed by the spirit of his dead child, Sun Myung Moon authorized the Black Heung Jin to travel the world, preaching and hearing the confessions of Unification Church members who had gone astray.

Confessions soon became central to the Black Heung Jin's mission. He went to Europe, to Korea, to Japan, everywhere administering beatings to those who had violated church teachings by using alcohol and drugs or engaging in premarital or extramarital sex. The Black Heung Jin spent a year on the road, dispensing physical punishment as penance for those who wished to repent, before Sun Myung Moon summoned him to East Garden.

We all gathered to greet him at Father's breakfast table. He was a thin black man of average height who spoke English better than Sun Myung Moon. He seemed to me intent on charming the True Family, in much the way a snake encircles and then swallows its prey. I was anxious to hear some concrete evidence that this man possessed the spirit of the boy I once knew. I was not to hear it. The Reverend Moon asked him standard theological questions that any member who had studied

the *Divine Principle* could have answered. He offered no startling revelations or religious insights. Maybe what most
impressed Father was his ability to quote from the speeches of
Sun Myung Moon.

The Reverend and Mrs. Moon suggested that we children
meet with the Black Heung Jin privately and report back to
them on our impressions. It was an amazing meeting. Hyun
Jin, Kook Jin, and Hyo Jin kept asking the stranger questions
about their childhood. He could not answer any of them. He
did not remember anything about his life on earth, he told us.
Instead of inspiring skepticism, the Black Heung Jin's convenient memory lapse was interpreted as a sign of his having left
earthly concerns behind when he entered the Kingdom of
Heaven. Everyone in the household embraced him and called
him by their dead brother's name. I avoided him and found
myself thinking that I was living with either the stupidest or
the most gullible people on earth. There was a third alternative
I did not consider at the time: the Reverend Moon was using
the Black Heung Jin for his own ends, just as he had used the
American civil liberties community before him.

Sun Myung Moon seemed to take pleasure in the reports
that filtered back to East Garden of the beatings being administered by the Black Heung Jin. He would laugh raucously if
someone out of favor had been dealt an especially hard blow.
No one outside the True Family was immune from the beatings.
Leaders around the world tried to use their influence to be
exempted from the Black Heung Jin's confessional. My own
father appealed in vain to the Reverend Kwak to avoid having
to attend such a session.

The Black Heung Jin was a passing phenomenon in the
Unification Church. Soon the mistresses he acquired were so
numerous and the beatings he administered so severe that
members began to complain. Mrs. Moon's maid, Won Ju

McDevitt, a Korean who married an American church member, appeared one morning with a blackened eye and covered with purple bruises. The Black Heung Jin had beaten her with a chair. He beat Bo Hi Pak — a man in his sixties — so badly that he was hospitalized for a week in Georgetown Hospital. He told doctors he had fallen down a flight of stairs. He later needed surgery to repair a blood vessel in his head.

Sun Myung Moon knew when to cut his losses. When you are the Messiah, it is easy to make a course correction. Once it became clear that he had to disassociate himself from the violence he had let loose on the membership, Sun Myung Moon simply announced that Heung Jin's spirit had left the Zimbabwean's body and ascended into Heaven. The Zimbabwean was not quite so ready to get off the gravy train. At last sighting, he had established a breakaway cult in Africa with himself in the role of Messiah.

8

I had just taken my last spring final exam at New York University when Hyo Jin called from Korea in May 1986. He had been in Seoul for weeks. He missed me and the baby, he said. We should come as soon as possible.

It was my first year in college. The Moons had been willing to send me on the theory that my academic success would reflect well on them one day. I had been up late every night for days, studying for finals and writing term papers. I wanted to do well, not only to justify the expense of my education to the Reverend and Mrs. Moon but to feel pride in my freshman accomplishments.

The classroom was the one place in my universe over which I felt complete mastery. I knew how to learn, how to study, how to take tests. I did not know how to think critically, but I rarely had to in order to earn good grades. The memorization skills I had learned as a child in Korea were serving me well in American higher education as well.

New York University had not been my first college choice. I wanted to attend Barnard College, the women's undergraduate division of Columbia University. I knew it was one of the prestigious Seven Sisters schools and I felt reassured that my classmates would be females. I was married and a mother but still as awkward as an adolescent girl around young men.

Barnard would not have me. I had foolishly applied as an early-decision candidate, a realistic option for only the very best students. My grades were good but my essays showed the lack of self-reflection that characterized my life at that time. I was determined after that initial rejection to do so well at N.Y.U. that Barnard would reconsider and accept me as a transfer student one day.

I was also in my first trimester of a new pregnancy when Hyo Jin summoned me to Seoul, and the prospect of the long flight with a toddler could not have been less appealing. I was worried, too, about the chance of miscarriage after my last, failed pregnancy. But it was so rare for Hyo Jin even to call me when he was away, let alone to request my company, that I eagerly interpreted this as a hopeful sign for our marriage.

The flight was every bit as grueling as I had feared. My daughter was too excited to sleep. She shook me every time I closed my eyes. I kept myself awake with optimistic thoughts of how God must have used this time to soften Hyo Jin's heart.

I was disabused of that fantasy as soon as my daughter and I arrived at the Moon household in Seoul. Hyo Jin had begged us to come and now he wanted nothing to do with us. I had become accustomed over the years to Hyo Jin's need to control me, but I was alarmed by his almost paranoid monitoring of my every movement while we were in Korea. When I told him I would like to look up some of my old friends from the Little Angels school, for example, he barked that I would do no such thing. "You have no friends," he told me. "I am your perfect friend. You do not need anyone else."

He would become enraged if he returned home and found that I had taken my daughter to visit my parents. It was my duty to be waiting when he came home. He made me so nervous that whenever I went to visit my mother, I called the Moon household each and every hour to see if he was looking for me.

The elder Moons had returned to New York from one of their frequent trips to Korea soon after I arrived in Seoul, but many of the older Moon children were in Korea. In Jin was among them. She had always been very close to Hyo Jin and had not cared for me from the moment we first met. She summoned me to her room a few days after my arrival in Korea. It was clear she was furious at me — for what, I did not know. We had only exchanged polite greetings in the hall.

I sat on the floor, appropriately humble before a True Child. "My brother is working so hard and what are you doing? Nothing!" she shouted. "You are lazy and spoiled. According to Korean tradition, you should be mopping the kitchen floor and washing the dishes. You rank in the lowest position in this family and you should be clear about that."

I was taken aback, but I knew In Jin did not expect me to answer. To have done so would have been impertinent. What was the point of telling her that Hyo Jin would not permit me to accompany him to church events? What would I gain by contradicting her? I let her fury wash over me. How often had I found myself in this position, on my knees being browbeaten by one of the Moons? It was difficult enough to hear the lies that they heaped upon me, but my powerlessness to respond reduced me to the status of a small child. Did In Jin really think that I preferred to live the life her brother forced on me? Did she think I would not enjoy seeing other people? Was she blind to how Hyo Jin spent his free time in Seoul?

The bar scene was even worse in Seoul than it was in New York. In Korea there was always someone willing to give Hyo

Jin money, always some old friend to join him in one or another of his many vices. My mother had asked my uncle Soon Yoo to keep an eye on him. My uncle was a smooth talker, a trumpet player who knew the nightclubs even better than Hyo Jin did. My mom had a soft spot for him because he was the little brother who had brought her shoes to her when my grandmother locked her in her room to prevent her from marrying my father. However, it was unclear who was watching whom when my husband and my uncle were together. After a drinking session, the two of them often visited a Seoul steam bath, where, I later learned, Hyo Jin had found a lover among the towel girls.

One night when Hyo Jin returned home from the bars, I was kneeling beside our bed in prayer, as I did every evening. I heard him come into the room, but I thought I should complete my prayer before greeting him. That was a mistake. His palm slammed into the side of my head. Because of my pregnancy, my balance was off. He knocked me over. "How dare you not rise to greet your husband," he said, his slurred words evidence that he was very drunk. "I was only trying to finish my prayer," I said in a foolhardy attempt to explain myself. Hyo Jin let loose with a string of complaints about me and my parents: I was an ugly, fat, and stupid girl; my parents were arrogant and disloyal to Father; they were an evil influence on me. When he went into the bathroom, I saw my opportunity and ran to another room. He was only a few steps behind me.

He began banging loudly on the door. I was terrified and worried his screaming would awaken our child. I huddled on the bed while her madman father tried to batter down the door, which I was grateful had a solid brass lock. After several minutes he left and I fell asleep. I woke the next morning to the sound of his cursing in the hall. This time he was wielding his guitar as a sledgehammer, but the heavy wooden door would not yield. When he left, I ran to another room.

No sooner had I slipped into a room down the hall than I saw him on the balcony outside. He smashed his guitar through the window, raining shards of glass down onto the chair where I had just been sitting. I ran down the staircase, the sound of his angry cursing in my ears. I took refuge in the rooms of a church leader who lived downstairs. Hyo Jin kept shouting for me to show myself. I was scared, but I wasn't stupid. I knew he would beat me senseless if I came out. I stayed hidden for hours while he recruited others in the household to search for me. When he finally gave up and went out to the bars, I called my father in hysterical tears. He immediately sent a car for my daughter and me.

It was the first time in my marriage that I was afraid for my life. Until then the abuse I had suffered had been more psychological than physical. I had spent years steeling myself against his cruelty and threats. I was "ugly" and "fat" and "stupid." Without him I was a "nobody" and a "nothing." I thought I was "so smart," but he was the son of the Messiah. I could be "replaced." I had trained myself not to react to his verbal abuse. At some level, I knew he was being defensive. Hyo Jin resented the education I was earning while he squandered his youth on booze and drugs and prostitutes. I knew not to fight back when he attacked me. To do so would only have invited more of the same. I worried for Shin June and the baby I carried, growing up in an atmosphere of such hatred and vitriol. For my children, I kept silent and tried not to offend him. It was like walking on eggshells; anything I said might set him off.

In many ways, Hyo Jin's abusive behavior was a natural response to the environment of coercion and control in the Moon household and the Unification Church. I, too, suffered under the restrictions the Moons imposed. The expectation that I would be available at a moment's notice to wait on Mrs. Moon meant I could have no substantive life outside the compound in Irvington. I was a phantom presence on campus when I attended New York University and, later, Barnard College.

Sun Myung Moon sent his children and sons and daughters-in-law to college to earn degrees that would bring greater public glory to him, not a broader personal experience to us. I made no friends for fear such contact would invite questions about my life or require further time away from the compound. Mrs. Moon already considered my studies a usurpation of time that rightfully should have been at her disposal.

I came and went from N.Y.U. with other Blessed Children. I interrupted my education to accommodate my pregnancies so often that I exhausted the number of leaves of absence each N.Y.U. student is allowed. In 1988, having earned high grades at N.Y.U., I transferred to Barnard. A security guard from East Garden would drive me to and from classes. Not even the professor who served as my adviser knew who I really was.

Much later, when I became pregnant with Shin Ok, my fourth child, I applied for a leave of absence from Barnard as well. My adviser, an older female professor, was very solicitous when I told her that I was pregnant. "Are you sure this is what you want?" she asked gingerly. "Oh, it's O.K. I'm married!" I laughed. What I didn't tell her was that Shin Ok would be my fourth child. I wasn't sure Barnard had ever seen a coed quite like me.

The books I read and the lectures I heard exposed me to wider views of the world, but for me it was all an intellectual exercise. In the stacks of Wollman Library at Barnard and of Butler Library at Columbia, I gained information, not insight. I had been trained all my life never to question, not to doubt.

No college course on the history of religion, no lecture on the roots of messianic movements, could have shaken my faith in Sun Myung Moon or the Unification Church.

The practical effect of blind faith is isolation. I was surrounded by people who believed as I did. Everything in my life — from my duty to prostrate myself before Mother and Father in greeting each morning to my duty to accept the divinity of my transparently flawed husband — reinforced that isolation. If I was angry or sad or upset, there was no one with whom I could share those feelings. The Moons did not care; my parents were a world away; and the staff of East Garden and ordinary church members barely spoke to me because of my elevated position as a member of the True Family.

I was alone. If not for prayer, I would have lost my mind. God became the friend and confidante I did not have on earth. He listened to my heartache. He heard my pain. He gave me strength to face my future with the monster I had married.

Hyo Jin's rage in Seoul frightened my parents. They knew I lived a difficult life in East Garden, but this was the first time they had seen my suffering up close. When I had arrived at their home with Shin June, I was still shaking and tearful. We knew Hyo Jin would come to get me, and my parents were powerless to defy the son of the Messiah. I was so scared he would beat me for running away. My father drove me to a hospital in Seoul, where doctors admitted me after we explained what had happened. Hyo Jin called my parents' home looking for me and demanded that I return. My father told him the doctors insisted I needed to stay in the hospital for the sake of the baby I was carrying.

It was not long before Hyo Jin appeared at my bedside. His message was clear: I could not hide out forever. I could not keep his daughter from him for long. I would have to come back eventually. He did not apologize or even acknowledge why I had fled the Moon household in terror. He wanted only to let me know that sooner or later I would have to return and face him.

I stayed in Seoul with my parents and my daughter for two months. Hyo Jin returned to East Garden. He explained my absence to his parents as an act of willfulness on my part. I was stubborn and defiant. He had had to hit me, he told them, because I had talked back to him. In their view, such physical punishment of a wife was justifiable. I remember one sermon at a 5:00 A.M. family Pledge Service when Father said wives should be struck now and then to keep them humble. "You wives who have been slapped or hit by your husband, raise your hands," he once instructed at a Sunday sermon at Belvedere. "Sometimes you may be struck because of your lips. The body's first criminal is the lips — those two thin lips!"

Unificationism teaches that wives are subservient to their husbands, just as children are subservient to their parents. They must obey. "If you beat your children from your temper, it is a sin," the Reverend Moon has said. "But if they do not obey you, you can bring them by force. It will be good for them, after all. If they do not obey you, you can even strike them." Just as Sun Myung Moon smacked his children when they defied him, the son of the Messiah felt free to beat his wife when she failed to accord him the respect to which he felt entitled.

A letter soon arrived for me at my parents' home from Mrs. Moon. She wrote to tell me that I must come back. It was wrong for me to be at my parents' house. I was not their child; I was Hyo Jin's wife. She was angry at my mother and father for sheltering me, anger that hardened against them when her own daughter Je Jin and my brother Jin sent their children to stay with my parents in Korea to shield them from the influence of the Moons. Je Jin and Jin were already having doubts about her parents and the church.

My parents and I both knew my time with them was no more than a temporary respite. I had to go back. It was my mission. It was my fate. It is easy for those outside the Unification Church to wonder how a mother and father could have sent their daughter back to an abusive husband and uncaring in-laws, but my parents and I believed we were fulfilling God's plan. It was not for us to alter that course. Even to consider leaving Hyo Jin Moon meant rejecting my life, my church, my God. For my parents, it meant questioning every decision of their entire adult lives.

Beyond my religious compulsion to return, there was my fear. A woman does not have to be trapped in a cult to feel powerless before the man who beats her. What battered woman has not heard a well-meaning friend or relative ask: "Why don't you leave?" It sounds so simple, but how simple is it for a mother of young children without resources who takes seriously her husband's threats to kill her? Women beaten by their partners are at their greatest risk of being murdered when they flee. Crime statistics confirm that reality but women know it instinctively. Even if I did not have the pressure of my faith forcing me back to East Garden, I had the pressure of my fear.

Leaving my parents' home that September was awkward and painful for all of us. I did not want to go. They did not want to let me. But none of us could see beyond the power of Sun Myung Moon and his church. There were tearful farewells with my mother and my siblings. My father could not even meet my gaze. I knew that his distress was as great as my own.

Hyo Jin did not come to meet Shin June and me at the airport. When we saw him at Cottage House, it was as though nothing had happened between us. At East Garden, Mrs. Moon summoned me to her room. She welcomed me home and assured me that Hyo Jin had promised there would be no repetition of the incident in Seoul that had kept me away so long.

She spoke in euphemisms about his violence and his substance abuse, reminding me that it was my duty to work as God's instrument to change her son. That was why I had been chosen. On the one hand, all my experience told me that her son was a pathological liar. On the other, I still believed in my divine mission, that God would bring about genuine change in him eventually if only I worked and prayed hard enough. I wanted to believe Mother's reassurances as much as every battered woman wants to believe her husband's promises to change.

Mrs. Moon was less indirect about her anger at my parents. It had been wrong of them to keep me in Seoul. She questioned their loyalty to Father. True Parents had been hearing reports from Korea about the Hongs that displeased them. I had only a vague idea of what Mrs. Moon was talking about. For some time my mother had been hinting that all was not well between them and the Reverend and Mrs. Moon. During recent visits of True Mother and True Father to Korea, the Reverend Moon had singled out my father for public criticism. He accused my father of packing Il Hwa with Hong relatives to the detriment of the company. He accused my father of taking credit for the success of Il Hwa when the success belonged to Sun Myung Moon.

My mother told me these things, but without alarm. Father was known for his perverse inclination to dress down those who actually pleased him. Only in the Unification Church could it be considered a compliment to be criticized in public. I would learn later, though, that the Reverend Moon had begun to take sadistic pleasure in humiliating my father in front of others. At the opening of a bottling plant whose design, financing, and construction my father had supervised, the Reverend Moon scoffed at him as an ineffectual executive who could be fired at the Messiah's whim. At his breakfast table in Seoul, he mocked my father in front of a dozen church leaders as a man led around by the nose by his wife.

It was difficult to know what accounted for the Moons' shift in attitude toward my parents. Sun Myung Moon was at once attracted and repelled by intelligence and competence. No one should ever appear smarter than the Messiah. My father had built a successful company from the ground up for the Reverend Moon. That was good; he had served his master well. My father had accomplished this through his own skill and hard work. That was bad; he might take credit for Il Hwa's success.

My mother was in an equally precarious position. A shy girl when she joined the Unification Church, she had become one of its most eloquent voices after years of preaching on Sun Myung Moon's behalf. Well read, she had become a respected voice on matters of religion. Mrs. Moon, who had not finished high school before she married Sun Myung Moon, was uncomfortable around well-educated and pretty women like my mother. She insisted on being introduced in public as Dr. Hak Ja Han Moon, but the title was an honorary one.

Mrs. Moon's insecurity was demonstrated by the kind of women she surrounded herself with in East Garden, Korean ladies I used to think of as her court jesters. They were there to entertain their mistress with jokes and foolishness, not to engage her in meaningful conversation. My mother was a breed apart. Smart and serious, she did not suffer fools. She was devoted to True Mother, but she did not play the role that Mrs. Moon most enjoyed.

The ladies around Mrs. Moon seized on her displeasure with my mother to further undermine her in True Mother's eyes. Many of these women were eaten up with jealousy that the Hongs had married into the True Family. Jin and I, in their view, had taken the rightful places of their sons or daughters.

Here was their opportunity for revenge. My mother's every action was distorted by the rumor mill. A gift of money to a church member in need was misinterpreted as an attempt to buy someone's affection. A defense of my father was read as an attack on the Moons.

In a medieval royal court, whoever whispered last into the ear of the king or queen had the most influence. It was no different in the Moon compound. The sycophants held sway. Soon there were rumors that my parents planned to establish a splinter church in Korea, that my father intended to declare himself the true Messiah. It was all nonsense, but the Moons were always willing to believe the worst. My father's role in the Unification Church steadily declined at the urging of Mrs. Moon. To lessen his impact in Korea, Mrs. Moon eventually had the Reverend Moon appoint my father as president of the Unification Church in Europe, the continent where the movement had the least influence in the world.

The Moons' mistrust of my parents spilled over into my life. I was told to minimize my contact with them. My calls through the East Garden switchboard to Korea were monitored to make certain that the Moons' directive was obeyed. To be cut off from my family was more isolation than I could stand. I installed a private telephone in my room to maintain ties to my mother and father.

Two months after I returned to East Garden, our second daughter, Shin Young, was born. There was the usual disappointment that I had not produced a male heir, but there was relief, as well, that Hyo Jin's abuse of drugs and alcohol had not damaged this beautiful baby girl.

A few months later, Mrs. Moon was preparing to return to Korea for an extended visit. She called me to her room and announced that she would be taking my four-year-old daughter with her to serve as a companion for her own five-year-old daughter, Jeung Jin. I did not dare voice my objections or ask all the questions I had. She did not indicate how long they would be gone. I barely had time to absorb this news when she returned from her closet safe with a Gucci handbag. It contained a hundred thousand dollars in cash. This was "seed money" for our family's future, she told me. I should invest it wisely, perhaps in gold. Later, she said, she would give us another three hundred thousand dollars. Was she bribing me? Taking my daughter away in exchange for cash?

I begged Hyo Jin to intervene with his mother. I knew my daughter would not want to go. Jeung Jin was spoiled, and her baby-sitter was mean. My daughter and I were very close. She would miss me terribly. She was too young for such a trip. Hyo Jin refused to speak with his mother. If our daughter was in Korea, it would give him a convenient excuse to go there himself and visit his girlfriends. Besides, there was the money to think about from his mother. I was advised to store it in a safe deposit box in a bank in Tarrytown. Had I deposited it in a savings account we would have to do the unthinkable: pay taxes on it. The safe deposit box was a mistake, of course. It provided Hyo Jin with ready access to cash. He used the money that was earmarked for our children's future to buy a thirty-thousand-dollar gold-plated gun for Father and motorcycles for himself and his brothers.

My little girl was in Korea for three long months. In the photographs Mrs. Moon sent home to East Garden, she was never smiling. When she left, she could hold a pencil and print her name. In Korea the baby-sitter slapped her hand and told her not to do that. Her aunt could not print her name, and the Moon children must be superior. It took me years to correct the damage. The baby-sitter would tell Shin June ghost stories that would give her nightmares. When she would ask to visit my mother, Mrs. Moon would distract her with a visit to a toy store or an ice cream parlor.

I vowed I would never let the Moons take any of my children from me again. The Moons brought the children on their speaking tours not because they loved their company but because they needed living ornaments, cutely outfitted decorations that would portray them as the loving parents and grandparents to the world. I would do whatever it took — flattery, manipulation, deceit — to stop Sun Myung and Hak Ja Han Moon from exploiting my children in the future.

My children were the one real blessing in my life. I defined myself as either pregnant or between pregnancies. I signed up for classes or dropped out of classes depending on my condition. In 1987 I was certain I was facing a second miscarriage. I was bleeding heavily in my fourth month. My doctor advised bed rest, but it did not stop the flow of blood. I was very frightened and I'm sure Hyo Jin heard as much in my voice when he called from Alaska, where he was fishing with his parents.

I was touched by the concern he expressed on the telephone but it had dissolved by the time he returned to East Garden. I was reading the Holy Bible in bed when he arrived at Cottage House. He knocked the Bible out of my hand. I put up my hands to protect myself from his blows. "Do you think the Bible is more important than True Parents?" he shouted. "Why weren't you outside to greet them?" I tried to explain about the bleeding and the doctor's orders but he was dismissive. If I was bleeding, then the baby was probably deformed, he yelled. It was better that I should miscarry than bring a damaged child into the True Family. I was appalled at his coldness. "Get up, you lazy bitch," he shouted.

I tried to do as he asked but I was too weak. I stayed in bed and he stormed out of the house. I called my mother in Korea, who promised to have her prayer group pray for me and the baby. Days later, when the bleeding still had not stopped, I concluded that the baby must be dead. I packed a bag for my trip to the emergency room, anticipating that I would have to stay overnight after having a D and C. At the hospital my doctor performed an ultrasound. I was so resigned to an unhappy ending that I had to ask her to repeat herself when she said that the baby's heartbeat was strong. The placenta had been bleeding, but it was beginning to heal.

That was the medical explanation, but I knew better. No baby could have survived the amount of blood I had lost. This was a miracle. When the doctor pointed out what else the ultrasound showed, I knew that this baby was a gift from God. I would bear a son. I told no one, not even my mother. When In Jin and Mrs. Moon asked later if I could tell the sex from the ultrasound, I said no. This was a secret between me and God. I felt that if I kept that secret, Satan would not try again to harm my baby.

The Moon household was ecstatic when I gave birth to Shin Gil on February 13, 1988. The Moons even softened temporarily toward my parents. Hyo Jin could not have been happier. A male heir strengthened his position as the rightful successor to his father. A son, the Reverend Moon hoped, would force Hyo Jin to accept his responsibilities to his family and to the Unification Church.

It was an idle hope. In April Hyo Jin made what was billed as a dramatic confession before a church gathering in the grand ballroom of the World Mission Center, the old New Yorker Hotel in New York City. It was Parents Day, a church holiday. "Many Blessed members blame Father for my wrongdoings. It is not Father's fault; it is my fault," Hyo Jin began. "It wasn't easy for me to come to America. It was a spawning ground for my hate and misunderstanding. People tried to explain, but I never listened. I had a lot of anger in my heart. I hated almost everybody."

He went on to detail his adolescent sexual encounters, his teenage drinking binges, his use of cocaine. But he led his audience to believe that these transgressions were all in his past. "I want to make sure none of these things happen to my brothers and sisters, to Blessed Children, to your children," he said. What he didn't say, of course, was that his drinking, his drug abuse, and his sexual promiscuity would continue unabated. "I want to do everything right from now on. That was the past and it comes and haunts me many times. I have told you everything, that I slept around, that I had many women. I have nothing more to tell you. Please forgive me."

It was quite a performance before the membership. Hyo Jin was crying; his brothers and sisters were embracing him. I was merely a spectator at this sideshow. In his confession he had never even mentioned my name. He apologized to God, to True Parents, to church members, but he had nothing to say to his wife.

I was not surprised when this speech was followed by a resumption of his dissipated lifestyle. He began insisting that I accompany him to karaoke bars and nightclubs. I sometimes went just to avoid a fight, but I hated the atmosphere. Hyo Jin could sleep all day, but I had to rise early with the children. I had classes to attend. His drunkenness repulsed me. He would drink a half bottle of tequila and then leave a $150 tip for the waitress. I would sip my Coke and watch the clock.

I was not good company but I could drive home. Hyo Jin inevitably ran into trouble when he tried to drive himself. In 1989 the Moons had purchased an Audi for me to drive back and forth to college. One night Hyo Jin took the car into the city. I got a call near midnight that he'd had an accident and needed me to pick him up at Amsterdam Avenue and 146th Street. I could guess why he was in Harlem; that's where he scored cocaine. He was not on the corner when I arrived so I drove around the area. I finally found him wandering several blocks away. He was drunk and incoherent. When I located the Audi, I was amazed that he had walked away uninjured. The car was a total loss.

With the insurance settlement, I leased a Ford Aerostar. It wasn't long before Hyo Jin borrowed that car as well. At 4:00 one morning, I was awakened by a call from the New York City police. Hyo Jin had been arrested for driving while intoxicated. We were expected at a birthday celebration that morning for one of the Moon children. I sent my children with the baby-sitter and drove to the precinct house on 125th Street. In the next two hours, I reclaimed my car and arranged for a lawyer to represent Hyo Jin at his arraignment. I returned to East Garden to face True Mother, who scolded me for failing to attend the breakfast banquet. "Where were you? Where is Hyo Jin?" she demanded. This was his mess, not mine. I was tired of covering for him. "Hyo Jin is not here. When he comes home, I think you should ask him directly," I said.

Hyo Jin returned to East Garden incensed that I had not gotten him released from jail sooner. He was furious to be told that Mother was waiting for him. He needn't have been. The Moons took no action against their wayward son. The criminal justice system fined him, suspended his license, and ordered him to perform community service, but his parents did nothing to stem his drinking and driving.

The next time he asked me to accompany him to the bars, I refused. "I can't go; I promised," I told him. "Promised who?" he demanded. "Myself," I said. He drove himself, without me and without his license.

Slowly I was learning to say no. More than any other factor, I think motherhood was responsible for my change in attitude. It was one thing to suffer the True Family's abuse myself; it was another to subject my children to it. I gave birth to my third daughter, Shin Ok, in October 1989. I was twenty-three years old, with four children and a miscarriage behind me. I did not know how many more babies lay ahead.

I could defy Hyo Jin's orders to accompany him to the bars, but I could not defy Mrs. Moon. In 1992 she told me I would accompany her on a ten-city tour of Japan. I was pregnant again, but I concealed my condition from my mother-in-law. My pregnancies were all that I had that were truly mine alone; I did not share them with the family of Sun Myung Moon until I had no choice.

The worshipful devotion accorded True Mother in Japan was beyond anything I had ever experienced in Korea. I had expected Mrs. Moon to be accommodated with the best hotel suites and the finest food, but what I saw in Japan was beyond pampering. Even her cutlery was kept separate, not to be used by anyone again, because it had touched True Mother's lips. The slavish attention given to Mrs. Moon by the Japanese may have reflected their longing for True Father, who is banned from Japan because of his tax conviction in the United States.

Japan could fairly be said to be the site of the first imperial cult. In the nineteenth century, the Japanese emperor was declared a deity and the Japanese people descendants of ancient gods. State Shintoism, abolished by the Allies in 1945 after World War II, required the Japanese to worship their leaders. Obedience to authority and self-sacrifice were considered the greatest virtues.

It was no wonder, then, that Japan was fertile fund-raising ground for a messianic leader like Sun Myung Moon. Eager young Unification Church members found elderly people anxious to ensure that their loved ones came to a peaceful rest in the spirit world. To that end, they fleeced thousands of people out of millions of dollars for religious vases, prayer beads, and religious pictures to guarantee that their deceased family members entered the Kingdom of Heaven. A small jade pagoda could sell for as much as fifty thousand dollars. Wealthy widows were conned into donating all of their assets to the Unification Church to guarantee that their loved ones would not languish in hell with Satan.

It was an extraordinary scene to witness. Church members waited on Mrs. Moon. Church leaders brought her stacks of money. At one juncture a member was styling my own hair when I noticed I had misplaced my watch. Within the hour a jeweler was in my hotel room with trays of expensive watches for me to choose from as a gift from our Japanese hosts. "Take several, take some for your family," the jeweler insisted. I was relieved when I found my own watch and was able to politely decline their generosity.

Japan's economy was booming. The country was fast becoming the source of most of Sun Myung Moon's money. In the mid-1980s church officials claimed the Unification Church was pulling in four hundred million dollars a year through fundraising in Japan alone. The Reverend Moon used that money for his personal comfort and to invest in businesses in the United States and around the world. In addition, the church owned many profitable enterprises in Japan itself, including a trading company, a computer firm, and a jewelry concern.

Moon explained Japan's crucial financial relationship to the Unification Church in theological terms. South Korea is "Adam's country" and Japan is "Eve's country." As wife and mother, Japan must support the work of Father's country, Sun Myung Moon's Korea. There was more than a little vengeance in this view. Few Koreans, including Sun Myung Moon and his followers in the Unification Church, have ever forgiven the Japanese for their brutal forty-year occupation of Korea.

Members of the family of Sun Myung Moon were thoroughly scrutinized by customs agents whenever leaving Korea or entering the United States. This trip was no exception. One benefit of her enormous entourage was that Mrs. Moon had plenty of traveling companions with whom to enter the country. I was given twenty thousand dollars in two packs of crisp new bills. I hid them beneath the tray in my makeup case. I held my breath in Seattle when customs agents began searching my luggage. I was the last of our party to go through customs, and the woman searching my bags seemed determined to find something. I pretended I did not speak English and could not understand her questions. An Asian supervisor came over and chastised her. "Can't you see she only speaks Korean," the supervisor said, smiling at me. "Let her through."

I knew that smuggling was illegal, but I believed the followers of Sun Myung Moon answered to higher laws. It was my duty to serve without question. I did what I was told, worrying more that I might lose the money than that I might be arrested. I was so grateful to God that they didn't find the money. In the distorted lens through which I viewed the world, God actually had thwarted the customs agents. God did not want them to find that money because that money was for God.

If I had thought about it with any critical sense, I would have realized that the money raised by street peddlers and pagoda sellers had little to do with God. Among other things, the money raised helped finance my husband's adolescent fantasies of being a rock 'n' roll star. With a group of church members, he had begun a recording career at Manhattan Center Studios, the church-owned facility next to the old New Yorker Hotel in Manhattan. The Reverend Moon bought the facility to promote a God-centered culture. The Metropolitan Opera, the New York Philharmonic, and Luciano Pavarotti recorded there. In 1987 Hyo Jin Moon began recording there, too. *Rebirth* was the name of the first album he cut, with second-generation Blessed Children Jin Man Kwak, Jin Hyo Kwak, Jin Heung Eu, and Jin Goon Kim.

Hyo Jin sold compact discs and tapes of his music to his only audience, the Unification Church, which included the Collegiate Association for the Research of Principles (CARP), which he served as the figurehead president. A campus student organization purportedly dedicated to world peace, CARP was just another recruitment arm and fund-raising tool of the Unification Church. Its most visible enterprise was the international Mr. and Miss University Pageant that CARP sponsored every year in different cities around the world.

Much of the money raised to do God's work was squandered on Sun Myung Moon's white elephant: the twenty-four-million-dollar personal residence and church conference center that he built on the grounds of East Garden. It took six years, and almost as many architects, to construct what might be the single ugliest building in Westchester County. We watched the building go through a dozen or more design changes and millions of dollars in cost overruns. What emerged was a stone and concrete monstrosity with a leaking roof.

The foyer and the bathrooms boasted imported Italian marble. The thick oak doors were carved with Korean flowers. There was a ballroom on the first floor and bedrooms for the Moons' many small children on the second floor, down the hall from their parents' lavish suite of private rooms. One of the two dining rooms had its own pond and waterfall. The kitchen was equipped with six pizza ovens. There was a third-floor game room and closets for Mrs. Moon's clothes the size of a conventional bedroom. There was a dentist's office and a turret that housed the office of Sun Myung Moon's secretary, Peter Kim. The building was a monument to excess and nonsense. A bowling alley was located, not in the basement, but on the third floor, right above Sun Myung Moon's bedroom. We used that room for storage. Hyo Jin, I, and the children moved into the mansion when True Parents moved into their new home.

At the end of 1992, Mrs. Moon told me I was to accompany her abroad again, this time on a European tour. I was battling exhaustion from my now advanced pregnancy and knew I would not be up to the demands of travel and waiting on True Mother. She and Hyo Jin were incensed when I declined to join her. What happened next, I know they saw as God's punishment for my defiance.

I was scheduled for an ultrasound in January 1993. I knew from his vigorous kicks that the baby was strong. I smiled at the flailing legs and arms on the ultrasound monitor. "Looks good," the doctor said as he ran the probe across my distended belly. Soon, however, the doctor's smile faded. "We have a problem," he said softly. His face was so troubled I knew I did not want to know the answer to the question I had to ask. "What's wrong?" A few seconds seemed like hours before he said, "This fetus does not have a brain." "What? How can the baby be kicking if it has no brain?" The kicks were only a reflex. The baby had no chance for survival outside the womb.

I cried so hard that the doctor led me out through a rear door. I'm sure I would have made a terrifying picture for the other pregnant women in the waiting room. I sat in my car for a long time before I was composed enough to drive home. When I came home, Hyo Jin was locked in the master suite. I knew what that meant. He was sniffing cocaine. I called my mom. I couldn't be specific. All I could say was: "There's something terribly wrong with the baby," whose kicks I could still feel in my womb.

My doctor and I agreed that it would be awful for my children if I gave birth to a baby we knew would not live. I got a second ultrasound from another doctor just to be sure that there was no mistake. I drove myself to the hospital where the abortion was to be performed. Hyo Jin did not want to come. The pain, and the terrible sense of loss, were more than I anticipated. I had to call and ask him to pick me up. He seemed annoyed at my tears during the silent drive home. I moved into Shin June's room. I was lonely and angry. Why had this happened? Had Hyo Jin's drug abuse caused this? Was God punishing me for failing to bring Hyo Jin back to him?

Mrs. Moon was upset because I had not shown up to serve them at table. I begged Hyo Jin not to tell his parents the details of our loss. It was personal. "Can't you just tell them I had a miscarriage?" I pleaded. In Jin had just had her fourth baby, and it was like a knife in my heart to hear her newborn crying in the house we shared. "You want me to lie to True Parents?" Hyo Jin asked indignantly. I only wanted some privacy, but I should have known that was too much to expect in the Moon compound. He told True Mother everything.

My secrecy enraged Mrs. Moon. It confirmed my untrustworthiness. I was duplicitous, a tool of my parents, who were trying to undermine the work of True Parents. The drumbeat of criticism against me and my parents became incessant. At Sunday-morning services, I would be vilified as the daughter of tools of Satan. I did not mind so much for myself but I hated for my children to have to listen to such ugly lies about their grandparents.

My mother and father were decent people who had devoted their lives, and the lives of their children, to Sun Myung

Moon. The reward for their misguided self-sacrifice was public scorn. In 1993 my father suffered a stroke and was removed by the Moons from his position as president of the Unification Church in Europe. He went home to Korea, where he was ostracized by the religious movement that he and my mother had helped build.

Hyo Jin was emboldened by Father's attacks on my parents. In response he stepped up his attacks on me. By 1993 Hyo Jin's use of cocaine was constant. He locked himself in our master bedroom suite for days on end, forcing me to keep extra clothes in my children's closets and to share their bedrooms.

One evening, after he had spent the entire week snorting cocaine and watching pornographic videos, he summoned me to his room but I refused to go. He came downstairs, screaming and yelling obscenities, into a room we used for church-related classes. He flipped the coffee table over onto its side and forced me into a corner of the room, pushing me up against the wall, his face only inches from my own.

I ran for the telephone to dial 911. "I'm calling the police," I warned, but he just slapped the phone out of my hand. "How dare you try to call the police on me?" he shouted. "They have no authority here. Do you think I'm afraid of the police? Me? The son of the Messiah?"

I did not know what he would do next, so I began shouting for help as loud as I could. The door to the classroom was wide open. I knew the security guards, the kitchen sisters, the baby-sitters, could all hear me. No one came. Who would have the nerve to stand up to Hyo Jin Moon? Who would protect me from the Messiah's son? He laughed at the futility of my screams and left the classroom in disgust. I called my brother Jin and told him I was going to the police.

I stumbled into the foyer in tears. There, huddled together on the staircase, were three of my four children. They were sobbing. "Don't leave, Mommy," they cried, as I headed for the front door. "I'll be right back. Don't worry," I whispered as I dried their tears.

I drove straight to the Irvington Police Department. Once I pulled into the parking lot, though, I didn't know what to do or why I had really come. I was still shaking, with fear and with rage. I sat there for a long time, praying for God to guide me. I had spent the last eleven years hiding my feelings, concealing the facts of my life from the outside world. What was I doing parked outside a police station? I was crying when the police officer looked up from the front desk. "I think I need some help," I said. He took me into a private back room and listened quietly while I told him what had happened. He recognized the street address. He knew the family name. I could tell he was not surprised.

Did I have any place to go? he wanted to know. Did I have any family? I had only my brother Jin, who was a student at Harvard. I did not want to involve Jin and Je Jin in this. She had her own problems with her parents; I did not want to drag her into mine.

The policeman was patient and kind. He described my options: I could file assault charges against Hyo Jin; I could take my children to a shelter for victims of domestic violence. I thanked him but I knew in my heart that I could do no such thing. I was able only to file a report with the police. I did not lack the desire to flee; I lacked the courage. I was terrified to go back to East Garden, but sitting there in the Irvington police station, I was more certain than ever that I had nowhere to run.

9

By 1994 my only ambition was to see my children grown so that I could leave my husband. I knew that Sun Myung Moon would never permit me to divorce Hyo Jin, but I fantasized that one day we could at least live apart. I dreamed of a time when I could live alone quietly in a small apartment, somewhere far from East Garden. The children would bring my grandchildren to visit me. I would be at peace.

It was a pathetic goal for a twenty-eight-year-old woman. I had just earned my undergraduate degree from Barnard College in art history, but I was writing off the next twenty-five years of my life. My passion for art, my vague thoughts of museum or gallery work, faded away, as dreamlike as the Impressionist paintings I favored.

In March I learned that I was pregnant again, and the joy I usually felt at the prospect of a new baby was this time mixed with dread. Each new birth would extend the length of my imprisonment.

It was a mystery to me how such precious lives could spring from such a poisonous union. It was my children who made me whole. With them I felt light and carefree. Their routines provided us with the only semblance of a normal life. I drove them to music and language lessons in a Dodge minivan just like other suburban moms; I helped them with their homework; I snuggled up with them at bedtime to read stories and to hear their daily concerns.

Too often, their worries were about their father. Nothing that went on in East Garden escaped the notice of our older son and daughters. Hyo Jin's drunken rages, his cocaine stupors, his volatile temper, were impossible for them to overlook. They were awakened in the middle of the night by the sound of us fighting. They questioned why their father slept all day. "Why do we have a bad dad?" the older ones would ask. "Why did you marry him?"

I was grateful that Hyo Jin stayed away as much as he did, working at Manhattan Center Studios and sleeping at our suite in the old New Yorker Hotel. It reduced the tension in the mansion, which we now shared with In Jin and her family. The children and I managed some happy, even silly, hours together. One spring I had taught myself to ride a bicycle in the mansion driveway, to the great amusement of my more competent children.

Manhattan Center, which was originally built in 1906 as the Manhattan Opera House by Oscar Hammerstein, had become the focus of Hyo Jin's life. The Unification Church had purchased the property, along with the New Yorker Hotel next door, in the 1970s. Manhattan Center was little more than a practice hall when Hyo Jin had taken charge of the production studios and the business operation in 1985. I was surprised that Sun Myung Moon had entrusted such a major enterprise to a son who had neither the education nor the experience — to say nothing of the discipline — to act as a chief executive officer. I should not have been. All over the world, when the Unification Church acquires new businesses, those enterprises serve as employment opportunities for the family of Sun Myung Moon.

For the first time in our marriage, for the first time in his life, Hyo Jin Moon at age twenty-six had a job. He supervised the production of videos for the church and he continued to record with his band of church members. I was no fan of rock music, but it was certainly true that Hyo Jin was a talented guitarist with a beautiful voice. He loved his music; it was the one unspoiled pleasure he had in life.

His employees at Manhattan Center were all members of the Unification Church, even though Manhattan Center Studios claims to be an independent corporation with no overt connection to the church. His employees accorded Hyo Jin the respect and loyalty due the son of the Messiah. With him they turned Manhattan Center into a sophisticated multimedia studio, with professionally run audio, video, and graphics departments. Hyo Jin's elevated spiritual standing made for strained work relations, however. Imagine answering to a boss you could not question, who interpreted any hesitation to carry out his orders as a sign of betrayal. It was a recipe for disaster.

Money flowed in and out of Manhattan Center in what could generously be described as a liberal and informal fashion. Some weeks employees did not get paid because Hyo Jin had earmarked the thousands of dollars sitting in the safe for the purchase of new equipment. Most lived rent-free in the New Yorker Hotel next door. When Manhattan Center's conventional sources of revenue — studio bookings and ballroom events — fell short, Hyo Jin would tap a church organization, such as CARP, to pay for a new video camera or the electricity bill. Personal "donations" to Hyo Jin financed the building of new studios and recording facilities. Church funds, channeled to Manhattan Center from True Mother, were recorded on the books as "TM."

Manhattan Center became the fuel that powered Hyo Jin's moral collapse. It was a source of ready cash to finance his cocaine habit, his growing arsenal of guns, and his nightly drinking binges. Manhattan Center provided Hyo Jin, who hated to drink alone, with a stable supply of drinking companions, all of whom had no choice but to attend to this True Child.

Most members of the Unification Church get no closer to the True Family than the distance between the stage and their seats at some rally. For the staff of Manhattan Center, the opportunity to work directly with Hyo Jin Moon was a matter of great pride. It soon became a source of spiritual conflict for many of them, however. He would order his inner circle to accompany him to Korean bars in Queens, where he cavorted openly with "hostesses" and drank himself senseless. He pressured people to take cocaine, people who had been drawn to the Unification Church because of its prohibitions against the very acts of self-destruction in which Hyo Jin was engaged.

As his cocaine abuse escalated, so did his belligerent behavior toward his staff and his family. His verbal abuse of me had grown from obscenity-laden insults to threats of physical harm. He would open the gun case he kept in our bedroom and stroke one of his high-powered rifles. "Do you know what I could do to you with this?" he would ask. He kept a machine gun, a gift from True Parents, under our bed. At Manhattan Center, those who displeased him became accustomed to hearing graphic descriptions of the violence that would come to them if they betrayed Hyo Jin Moon. An accomplished hunter, he once detailed for a gathering of his inner circle exactly how he would like to skin and gut a member of his staff who had recently left Manhattan Center.

It is difficult for anyone outside the Unification Church to understand the bind those close to Hyo Jin at Manhattan Center found themselves in. On the one hand, their leader was engaging in activities that were inimical to their beliefs. On the other hand, he was the son of the Messiah. Perhaps he had some special dispensation to act as he did. If they did not obey and join him in proscribed behavior, were they substituting their own inferior judgment for that of a True Child? Should they be honest with the Messiah or loyal to the son of the Messiah? Would they be protecting Hyo Jin Moon by exposing him or by shielding him?

Even if one or more of them had had the independence of mind to question Hyo Jin's actions, unlikely given the authoritarian nature of the church, who would they have told? One doesn't just call up East Garden and ask to speak to Sun Myung Moon. Even if a member tried to make an appointment to see Mrs. Moon, that information would soon be public knowledge. Hyo Jin would not have been pleased to discover that one of his trusted advisers had gone to True Parents to inform them that their son was an alcohol-abusing, drug-addicted womanizer.

On the contrary, the inner circle had enough experience with Hyo Jin's unpredictable temper to go to any lengths to appease him. He terrorized his workers, reminding them whenever they displeased him that he was "a mean son of a bitch," one of his favorite self-descriptions.

No one was learning that better than I. In September Hyo Jin beat me severely after I found him taking cocaine with a family member in our bedroom at 3:00 A.M. I could not contain my anger. "Is this how you want our family to live?" I asked him. "Is this the father you want to be to our children?" I told him I could not live like this anymore. I tried to flush the cocaine down the toilet, spilling some on the bathroom floor in the process. He pushed me to the floor and made me sweep up what white powder I could retrieve. He smashed his fist into my face, bloodying my nose. He wiped my blood on his hand and then licked it off. "Tastes good." He laughed. "This is fun."

I was seven months pregnant at the time. While he punched me, I used my hands to shield my tummy. "I'll kill this baby," Hyo Jin screamed and I could see he meant it.

The next morning my tearful children gave me ice for my blackened eye and hugs for my battered spirit. I can't say Hyo Jin hadn't warned me. How often had he told me that there was a deep well of violence inside him? "If you push me too far, I won't be able to stop myself," he would say. I knew now that he was not exaggerating.

Hyo Jin felt no regret for the beating he had administered. He told his inner circle at Manhattan Center later that he smacked me because I had been "bugging" him and that I reminded him of a teacher he had once had at school, who always tried to humiliate him in front of the class. I was a pious scold, he said, a self-righteous bitch.

As strong as his contempt was for me, it did not approximate his hatred of his Father. He loathed and loved Sun Myung Moon in equal measure. He mocked him in front of me and in front of his associates at Manhattan Center as a senile old fool who should know his time to leave; he denounced him as an uncaring father who had never had time for his children. He blamed his father for the taunts of "Moonie" hurled at him by his American classmates when he was a boy. He resented the burden of being the heir apparent to the Unification Church, but he chafed even more at his own inability to live up to his father's expectations. He kept a gun at Manhattan Center, whose security chief often purchased weapons for him. When he was high, Hyo Jin would wave the gun around wildly and threaten to shoot his father if Sun Myung Moon ever tried to interfere with his control of Manhattan Center.

That control was absolute. He used Manhattan Center money as if it were his own and had his own paycheck deposited into a joint account with Rob Schwartz, his financial adviser at the company. Manhattan Center was there to serve his every whim. In 1989 and again in 1992, he had instructed Schwartz to buy a new Mercedes for Father with company funds. On another occasion he purchased an eighteen-foot fishing boat and trailer for the use of the extended Moon family. What those cars and that boat, all of which were kept at the compound in Irvington, had to do with the business of Manhattan Center was anyone's guess.

The casualness with which Hyo Jin mingled his personal funds and church money and business accounts would have intrigued the Internal Revenue Service. In 1994 he ordered Rob Schwartz to give one of his younger sisters thirty thousand dollars. There was internal debate at Manhattan Center about how best to disguise this transfer of funds. In the end, proceeds from the Mr. and Miss University Pageant held at Manhattan Center were kept off the books and thirty thousand dollars was handed to Hyo Jin to give to his sister. The year before, a group of Japanese members of the Unification Church was touring the United States. On a visit to Manhattan Center, they made a personal "donation" to Hyo Jin of four hundred thousand dollars in cash. He kept some of the money and used the rest for pet projects at Manhattan Center. He never reported the gift on his tax return or paid a dime of taxes on the money.

In February 1994 Hyo Jin carried a Bloomingdale's shopping bag into Manhattan Center containing six hundred thousand dollars in cash. I had helped him count out the money earlier in the day in our bedroom. He gathered his inner circle of advisers in his office, and while their jaws dropped open, Hyo Jin asked if they had ever seen so much money. What he didn't tell them was that he had skimmed off four hundred thousand dollars for himself of the one million dollars Father had given him to finance Manhattan Center projects. Hyo Jin stashed the money in a shoebox in our bedroom closet. By November he had spent it all, mostly on drugs.

It is probable that Sun Myung Moon did not know until November of 1994 the extent to which Hyo Jin had turned Manhattan Center into his personal petty cash drawer and the family suite on the thirtieth floor of the New Yorker into his private drug den. He did not know because he did not want to know. The Reverend and Mrs. Moon had set the tone for their parental relationship with Hyo Jin back when he was a boy, expelled from school for shooting at classmates with a BB gun. On that occasion, and in every troubling incident since, they had not forced their son to accept responsibility for his actions. He grew up believing that there were no consequences for his misdeeds, and his parents, and the church hierarchy, did nothing to disabuse him of that notion.

That fall, for instance, Hyo Jin had been a guest speaker in a course called Life of Faith at the Unification Theological Seminary in Barrytown, New York, where he was enrolled as a part-time student. Another student asked Hyo Jin a general question about his remarks and Hyo Jin took offense. Without a word he walked over to where the student was seated and began punching him. The student remained seated and did not strike back.

Hyo Jin received two letters from Jennifer Tanabe, the academic dean, after the incident. One was a joint letter of reprimand to Hyo Jin and the student he assaulted, Jim Kovic; the other was a personal note to Hyo Jin advising him to disregard the official letter. "Please understand that my intention in addressing this letter to you, as well, is not to accuse you but to protect you against any possible accusation. I will do my very best to support you. This is my determination before God," she wrote, incredibly ending her note with an apology to a man who had beaten up a student in one of her classrooms. "I am sorry to bring such bad memories of your experience at UTS. I hope that in the future you will find UTS to be some-where that can bring you joy and inspiration."

By November Hyo Jin was about to run out of excuses and defenders. The month began with the birth of our second son and fifth child, Shin Hoon. Hyo Jin was out at the bars when I went into labor, so I drove myself to the hospital with the baby-sitter in the passenger seat. I wanted her to learn the way so that she could bring the other children to visit me and their new brother. Before we left I put the children to bed. I told them I was going to the hospital to have the baby and that they should go to school the next day without telling any-one where I was. My desire for privacy in the suffocating world of the Moon family had become paramount. I called my brother Jin in Massachusetts to let him know I was on my way to Phelps Hospital and to ask him to call our parents in Korea.

I didn't care that Hyo Jin was not with me. This was my baby, mine and my children's. He had nothing to do with us as a family. If he preferred the company of barmaids, why should he be there for the birth of my son? At 4:00 A.M., when I was told I needed a cesarean section, my doctor insisted I call my husband. He was asleep. He assumed I was in one of the chil-dren's rooms down the hall. He urged me to come and service him sexually. He was startled to hear that I was about to be wheeled into the operating room.

He was too tired to come, he said. "What hospital is it anyway?" he asked. This was our fifth child and he did not know where they were all born? I was enraged. I did not answer. Hyo Jin began yelling. I hung up, but after I calmed down, I called back. "Forget it," he said coldly. "I'm not coming. You can bring the baby to me."

I saw my first glimpse of "Hoonie" through my tears. A nurse kept wiping my eyes as the doctor lifted this big boy, almost nine pounds, from my womb. He had a full head of black hair. The umbilical cord had been wrapped around his arm, complicating a natural delivery. His eyes were half closed but he had a healthy wail.

Hyo Jin did not come to see him for two days. His pride and his indifference kept him away. I was as stubborn as Hyo Jin, but I called to ask him to see his son. He stayed for only a few minutes with me and viewed Shin Hoon through the nursery window. He never asked to hold him. That night the baby-sitter brought my children. I was so happy to see them. They all posed for pictures with their new baby brother and begged me to come home soon.

I came home the next day, though the doctors wanted to keep me longer because of the surgery. I did not want anyone in the Moon compound to know I had had a cesarean section. It was such an anomaly to be in possession of information the Moons did not have; I wanted my surgery to be my secret. Hyo Jin came with the children and the baby-sitter in two cars to pick us up at the hospital. When it took longer than he had patience for to adjust the infant seat, he took off with Shin Gil for home, leaving me to ride with the baby-sitter. That night Hyo Jin announced he was going to New York. What I did not learn until later was that my husband had chosen the very day I brought our baby home from the hospital to take a lover. He slept with Annie, an employee at Manhattan Center, in our bed in our suite in the old New Yorker Hotel.

I knew Annie from the dozens of letters she had written to Hyo Jin since she first saw him at a church martial arts demonstration in Colorado several years before. Her letters read more like fan mail than anything else. Hyo Jin often got similar letters from young people in the church, men and women, who looked up to him as the son of the Messiah. I never took Annie's infatuation with Hyo Jin seriously. An American herself, she was married to a Korean member and they had a young son. Annie had come to New York that year to work for Hyo Jin at Manhattan Center after appealing to him to bring her and her husband back from Japan, where they were stationed for the church.

Hyo Jin talked about her often, but I did not suspect the nature of their relationship initially. Maybe I did not want to see what was becoming more and more obvious to everyone else around them. I worried more about his dependence on cocaine. He was closeted in his room all the time that he was not at Manhattan Center. As it turned out, I was not alone in my concern.

Twenty-one days after the birth of a child, we hold a prayer service in the Unification Church to give thanks to God for the health of our baby. I held an informal service with my children. Hyo Jin had been out drinking all night and had not returned. His sister Un Jin came by that afternoon to see the baby. We had not been close for years, but I would never forget the kindnesses she showed me when I first came to East Garden.

She confided that she was worried about Hyo Jin. He had lost a lot of weight. He wasn't eating. Did I think his problems with booze and drugs had gotten worse? Did I think True Parents should send him to rehab? I told her what I saw of his deteriorating lifestyle, but I expressed skepticism that he would voluntarily confront his addictions.

The very next day, Hyo Jin threw a Thanksgiving party at Manhattan Center for the staff. He served wine. Only his inner circle really knew about Hyo Jin's drinking and cocaine use. The rest of the staff were shocked to see alcohol at a church function. When the Reverend Moon found out, he ordered the staff at Manhattan Center to meet with him, without Hyo Jin. He reminded them that Sun Myung Moon was the leader of the Unification Church; they were to support Hyo Jin by keeping him away from dangerous situations.

I called Hyo Jin's assistant, Madelene Pretorius, to find out how the meeting went. We did not know one another well. We had met only once, when she came to videotape the children at a school play. She told me what Father had said and admitted that they had not told the Reverend Moon or me the whole truth. He had asked them if they smoked or drank with Hyo Jin and no one had admitted it. The truth was, she said, that they smoked and drank with him all the time in bars and in our suite at the old New Yorker Hotel.

I was horrified. What he did to himself was bad enough, but to drag other church members into the sewer with him was unforgivable. That he used our apartment to engage in this behavior enraged me. This was the beginning of the end of my marriage, though I didn't know it then. Something in me was about to snap. I had accepted that it was my fate, my divine mission, to live a life of misery with this evil man. But I could not accept that the members of a church I still believed in were condemned to be led into sin by Hyo Jin's abuse of power.

I called him at Manhattan Center. I was much braver on the telephone than I would have been in person, where he might have beaten me. I told him on the telephone that I thought he was an animal, that the children and I did not want him to come home.

It was a shortsighted reaction on my part, because, of course, he did come home, and when he got there he came looking for me. In my fury, I had already cleaned out his closets, packed his bags, cut his pornographic videos into shreds, and stacked it all in the storage room down the hall. I heard the front door slam. He ran up the stairs, grabbed me by my shirt collar, and dragged me into his room. He pushed me roughly into a chair, shoving me back down whenever I attempted to stand. "How dare you try to embarrass me in front of people at M.C.?" he screamed. "Who are you to tell me what to do?" He stood over me, slapping me and pushing me the whole time. I had no avenue of escape.

I was saved only because he was late for a meeting with his probation officer. He was still on probation for drunken driving. He tried to call and cancel the appointment, pleading a family emergency, but his probation officer insisted he come. He had missed too many appointments. "When I get back, I want a family meeting," he told me. "You are going to tell the children that you were wrong to criticize Dad, that Dad is free to smoke and drink beer, that you are a bad mother. Do you understand?" I said that I did. I would have said anything to get him to leave.

No sooner had he gone than I got a telephone call from Mrs. Moon's maid. "Father wants to see you right away," she said. I thought I was about to be lectured again for failing to help my husband find a righteous path. I had had enough; it was time for me to take the initiative. The rising level of abuse had emboldened me somehow. I had not consciously decided that I was not going to take his beatings anymore, but that night, in the Moons' study, I stood up for myself for the first time.

"Father wants to speak with you," Mrs. Moon said as I

entered their suite. "Could I please talk with you both?" I asked. "There is something I need to tell you."

The Reverend and Mrs. Moon listened in silence as I described the scene that had just transpired. "It is not just me and the people at M.C. who are being affected," I said. "Hyo Jin wants me to tell the children that his use of alcohol and drugs is O.K." That was enough to spark a reaction in Father. "No. No," he said, "you have to teach the children right from wrong." I kept looking at my watch. I told True Parents I needed to get back before Hyo Jin did from his meeting with his probation officer.

The Reverend Moon was quiet for a few minutes: "I am going to send you to M.C. to keep an eye on him. You are to be his shadow. I will put you in charge. You can make sure he does not use money for drugs and drinking."

I was surprised, but I knew that his use of me as his eyes and ears at Manhattan Center had less to do with his faith in my ability than with his certainty of my loyalty. The staff at Manhattan Center owed an allegiance to Hyo Jin; I followed True Father. He was right in the short run. In the long run, as we were all to discover, I realized that my ultimate loyalty was to God, my children, and myself.

When I returned to the mansion, Hyo Jin had not yet returned. I called our oldest child to my room. "Dad wants a family meeting," I told her. "I'm going to have to say some things I don't believe, because otherwise your dad will get very angry." She was appalled that I would even consider saying what he demanded. "You are not a bad mom. You are a good mom. You can't say what he does is O.K. when you know that it isn't." I could see that she was disappointed in my willingness to compromise the truth. I was ashamed in front of my twelve-year-old daughter, whose sense of justice was finely honed at a young age.

I was selfish. I wanted to avoid more violence, more scream-ing. When he returned and asked me to tell the children I had been unfair to Dad, I did it. My daughter's eyes filled with tears, but she was not sad. She was angry. "That's a lie," she yelled at her father. "Mom is good. She is with us all the time. You are never here. What do you know?" Hyo Jin turned his fury on her, denouncing American schools for breeding disre-spectful children.

I felt like a coward witnessing my little girl's courage. When Hyo Jin calmed down, he told her he had to spend time away from the family to pursue his mission for the church. I could not help but think of the irony: this was the excuse he had so despised when it came from his own father.

I was surprised that, despite his angry protests, Hyo Jin accepted my new role at Manhattan Center. He did not suspect why Father had placed me there, and since he had so little respect for me, he probably thought my presence would be no threat to him. He soon learned otherwise. As one of my first directives, I set up a meeting between Hyo Jin's inner circle and Sun Myung Moon at East Garden. The Reverend Moon told them as explicitly as he could that they were not to take drugs with Hyo Jin or to drink with him. They were to give their allegiance to Father, and at Manhattan Center they were to follow my directions, not Hyo Jin's.

As angry as I was at Hyo Jin, I was still susceptible to his accusation that it was my lack of understanding and support as a wife that led him to drink and abuse drugs.

If I was responsible in some way, I had to try one more time, with all my heart, to make things right, if not for us then for God. I spent all of my free time in December in Hyo Jin's com-pany. I went with him everywhere. I sat with him at home while he snorted cocaine.

The drug loosened his tongue and I listened for hours to his stream-of-consciousness pronouncements about God and Satan and Sun Myung Moon. The more I heard, the more convinced I became that Hyo Jin had no real sense of right and wrong. It was sad to hear him devise pathetic excuses, to tailor his morality to suit his circumstances.

His drug-induced monologues invariably portrayed him as the victim of his parents' neglect, of his wife's harsh judgment, of the church's unrealistic expectations. I listened for any hint that my husband was capable of taking some responsibility for the bad choices he had made and was continuing to make.

I heard nothing of the kind. All of Hyo Jin Moon's problems were the fault of others. As long as that was his attitude, how could he ever really serve God? How could he ever really be a good father to our children?

At Manhattan Center I set about trying to get the company's financial and spiritual house in order. I instructed Hyo Jin's assistant, Madelene Pretorius, that there were to be no more "petty cash" payments of hundreds of dollars at a time to Hyo Jin. Staff members who were paid huge salaries for little work were to be reassigned. All major decisions would have to be approved by me.

I had another mission at Manhattan Center as well. I was determined to find out whether Hyo Jin and Annie were lovers. Madelene suspected they were. Even my brother-in-law Jin Sung Pak had hinted there was something going on between them. I asked Hyo Jin directly many times, prompting the denials I expected but did not believe. After I began working at Manhattan Center, he taunted me about their ambiguous relationship. "Why do you worry about Annie?" he would ask, as if he were baiting me.

At the end of December, I decided I would hammer away at this topic until he confessed. It took hours of gentle coaxing for the truth to emerge. "No, I did not touch her," he insisted at first. "Well, maybe I kissed her," he conceded. "Maybe we had oral sex." His rationalizations got more strained the more impropriety he was willing to admit. "I did penetrate her, but I didn't ejaculate so it doesn't count," he said, before finally confessing: "I did ejaculate, but it doesn't matter because she is on the pill." I wondered if this guy even knew how pathetic he sounded.

I was very calm as he described his betrayal of our family. I had known in my heart all along; his confession was just confirmation. He began to cry and beg my forgiveness. I told him I would try to forgive but that I would not sleep with him until he had paid for his sin. "Why Annie?" I asked impulsively. "She's not even that pretty." It was as if I had held a match to gasoline. He exploded in rage: "She's beautiful!" he yelled. "She's not the only one. All the women in the church want me. I'll fuck the prettiest girl I can find. I'll show you."

I was numb. This was the man who claimed to be the son of the Messiah, a man who had stood up at a church service a few years before and preached about the sacredness of the Blessing. "How can you connect to the Messiah if you are indulging and wallowing in the sensuality of the fallen world? You can't. That's why the idea of sacrifice has been promoted and endorsed," he had told a Sunday-morning gathering at Belvedere.

"If Father told you to go out of this room and go to bars, get loaded and go to the streets where prostitutes walk and dwell among them, are you strong enough, do you love Father enough to overcome the kind of temptation that you might or might not expect there? Could you keep your purity and integrity? Could you truly do that? Living in that environment for the sake of changing the people is a good reason for living there. But do you know Father enough to overcome the temptation of touching a woman, of looking at beautiful women, or

being intoxicated where your ability to make a sensible decision becomes weaker and weaker? Under that circumstance
can you hold on to Father? Are you strong enough not to abandon Father regardless of the circumstances?"

I knew now that Hyo Jin Moon was addressing those questions not to the members but to himself and the answer, sadly,
was no. Continuing the pattern that had defined his life, Hyo
Jin refused to take responsibility for his adultery, the single
worst sin in the Unification Church. He told me, as I later
learned he had told Annie and his inner circle, that the
church's sexual prohibitions did not apply to him. Father had
been unfaithful; as the son of the Messiah, he could be, too.
His sexual liaisons were "providential," or ordained by God.

"I trusted Hyo Jin who said 'I know what I'm allowed to do.'
He never even gave me a hint that I would be falling with him,"
Annie would write me later. "Madelene told me some story
about Father having a relationship outside of Mother and a son
being born. This was later confirmed to me by Hyo Jin and Jin
Sung Nim. We discussed if it could be true and what it meant. I
never questioned Father's purity or his course. But I certainly
began to feel that there must be a lot going on providentially
within the True Family that I can't understand or judge."

I went directly to Mrs. Moon with Hyo Jin's claims. She was
both furious and tearful. She had hoped that such pain would
end with her, that it would not be passed on to the next generation, she told me. No one knows the pain of a straying husband like True Mother, she assured me. I was stunned. We had
all heard rumors for years about Sun Myung Moon's affairs and
the children he sired out of wedlock, but here was True
Mother confirming the truth of those stories.

I told her that Hyo Jin said his sleeping around was "providential," and inspired by God, just as Father's affairs were.
"No. Father is the Messiah, not Hyo Jin. What Father did was

in God's plan." His infidelity was part of her course to suffer to become the True Mother. "There is no excuse for Hyo Jin to do this," she said.

Mrs. Moon told Father what Hyo Jin was claiming and the Reverend Moon summoned me to his room. What happened in his past was "providential," Father reiterated. It has nothing to do with Hyo Jin. I was embarrassed to be hearing this admission from him directly. I was also confused. If Hak Ja Han Moon was the True Mother, if he had found the perfect partner on earth, how could be justify his infidelity theologically?

I did not ask, of course, but I left that room with a new understanding of the relationship between the Reverend and Mrs. Moon. It was no wonder she wielded so much influence; he was indebted to her for not exposing him all these years. She had made her peace with his faithlessness and betrayal. Perhaps all the money, the world travel, the public adulation, were compensation enough for her.

They would not be enough for me. For once Hyo Jin Moon was going to see that every action brings a reaction, that for every misdeed there is a consequence to be faced. I received the Reverend and Mrs. Moon's permission to send Annie away. But first I gave her the chance to tell the truth. I wanted her to admit what she had done to me, to her husband, and to God. She vowed in the name of True Parents that she and Hyo Jin had done nothing wrong.

After I had banished her from Manhattan Center, she wrote to me from her parents' home in Maine. Her husband had taken their son and returned to Japan. He wanted a divorce. "Now, I can taste your pain, your anguish and your tears . . .," she wrote, suddenly contrite and begging my forgiveness. She wrote several more times, describing her sex life with my husband in more detail than I needed to read, claiming to accept responsibility for what she had done.

There is no Feast of the Epiphany on the Unification Church calendar, but I had my own epiphany one day in January of 1995. The seeds of my emancipation had been sown that fall when Hyo Jin had his blatant affair and flaunted his drug use in front of church members. On a cold mid-January day I had one of those moments of revelation that I had only read about. Hyo Jin was dressing to go out to the bars for the evening. The events of the last few months had done nothing to alter his habits. I watched from a chair in the master bedroom as he stared at his reflection in the full-length mirror. He had always been very vain. But as he tucked in his shirt and fussed with his hair, I felt a detachment I had never experienced in my marriage. Even my revulsion was gone.

There was no voice from on high, there was no blinding light from above. I just knew: God no longer expected me to stay. My husband would never change. God himself had given up on Hyo Jin Moon. I was free to go. I was overwhelmed with a spirit of well-being. For Hyo Jin I felt only pity. He was a lost soul who had no conception of right and wrong and no real understanding of God.

It is a long road from resolution to action for a battered woman and one that few of us are able to walk alone. I was lucky I did not have to. Madelene Pretorius hardly knew me. She had worked for Hyo Jin for three years. She was an unlikely ally. That winter she spent her days listening to Hyo Jin complain about me in the office and her nights listening to me complain about him on the telephone. She was torn between her loyalty to the divine son of the Messiah and her recognition of the very human, abusive man we both knew. Hadn't Hyo Jin once thrown an ashtray at her head in a barroom? Hadn't he doused her with water when a bottle he threw at her crashed on the wall above her chair?

She was the first person outside my family I had ever been

able to talk to about my feelings. Even with my family, I hid more than I revealed about my life. I did not want to hurt them by letting them know the extent of the abuse my children and I were enduring. Madelene listened with a patience and concern I had never known. I had never had a real friend. I don't pretend that in those early months I was a friend to her. But she was to me. It would be a long time before I stopped acting like an officious member of the True Family and she stopped acting like a subservient member of the Unification Church. But even at the beginning, I saw a glimpse of what an honest relationship between equals could really be like.

At the time, Madelene was going through a personal crisis of her own. She had been matched and married through the church to an Australian man. She cared for him but did not want to follow him when he decided to return to his homeland. She struggled with her decision. Divorce is a creation of man; the Blessing is eternal. Unificationists believe that you remain mated even after death, in Heaven. It was revealing that Hyo Jin encouraged her to divorce; his self-interest in keeping her working at Manhattan Center was stronger than his commitment to a central tenet of his faith.

I wish I could say I helped her through her ordeal, but I was too wrapped up in my own problems, too inexperienced at friendship to really understand its reciprocal nature. It is a measure of the kindness Madelene showed to me that she was willing to help me without any expectation that I could help her in return. Madelene went home to South Africa for a month to make some decisions about her own life. When she returned in late February, she told me that she was getting a divorce and I told her I was leaving Hyo Jin.

Once I had made up my mind to go, I knew it was just a matter of time, but I was surprised to hear myself say the words out loud. Madelene and I talked in the laundry room in the basement of the mansion at East Garden so that Hyo Jin would not see us. He was so possessive and controlling that he erupted whenever he thought I was forming an attachment to anyone outside the True Family.

I began to cry as we talked. I said I hoped we could stay in touch after I left, though I knew that might be difficult for her. Madelene was saddened, but not surprised, by my news. She said that a part of her wanted to tell Hyo Jin, to try to shake him into seeing what he was about to lose. She would not do that, she said, because it would only have provoked him to beat me again or to issue one more false promise to change. We both knew my marriage was beyond saving. I had been seduced so many times into believing that God would touch Hyo Jin's heart or that Sun Myung Moon would exercise some moral leadership in his own household. It was not to be. I was at the end of the line.

That spring, Hyo Jin's behavior only worsened. Father had prohibited him from returning to Manhattan Center for two years, until he got his addiction problems under control. Hyo Jin called Manhattan Center and threatened to come down and smash the studio equipment. He was still being paid, of course. The Moons called it a disability payment, even though the company carried no disability insurance on its employees. Hyo Jin, in the meantime, was doing nothing to address his substance abuse. He would not enroll in a drug rehabilitation program; he would not see a therapist. If anything, he was spending more time closeted in his room, using cocaine and drinking. He would send Shin Gil to the refrigerator for beer and then lock himself in his room. For the sake of my children, I knew I could not remain in this environment much longer.

The final straw came when True Parents told me they thought that Hyo Jin was ready to return to Manhattan Center.

He was bored at East Garden and needed productive work. Hyo Jin's first project when he returned to Manhattan Center, he told me, would be to make an international singing sensation out of a bar girl who entertained at a Korean club in Queens. I knew the Moons were making a terrible mistake, that Hyo Jin was in worse shape than ever and a return to Manhattan Center would just broaden his opportunities to drink and use cocaine. I had my own suspicions about his real intentions toward the Korean bar girl. I knew the Moons would not listen to me. In April they did listen to concerned church members who wrote to protest Hyo Jin's reinstatement in his old job.

> *Dearest True Parents,*
>
> *On behalf of all the members of Manhattan Center, we the leaders and department heads come before you with a humble heart of repentance for our inability to create an environment that could support and protect Hyo Jin Nim and assist him in fulfilling his historical responsibility.*
>
> *We wish to express our loyalty and support to our True Parents at this very crucial time, and wish to convey the following key points:*
>
> *1. Our primary desire is to ensure that Manhattan Center is a place that can be completely claimed and used by God, True Parents and the worldwide Unification movement.*
>
> *2. That as such, we absolutely pledge to uphold True Parents' tradition and to maintain and substantiate that standard as the force that guides the lives of all members in the mission at Manhattan Center. We also realize that only through connecting M.C. to True Parents' greater vision do our efforts have any value at all.*

3. That on this foundation we wish to express our heart of love for Hyo Jin Nim, and the desire to support and help him in fulfilling his position and responsibility.

4. Therefore, based on this heart, we absolutely do not want M.C. to be a place that Hyo Jin Nim can use to make his problems worse. We want to be totally sure that he is protected from using M.C. in any way that may bring greater harm to himself and to the spiritual lives of members, to the growing business foundation, or to the reputation and foundation of the Church.

5. We therefore wish to support our True Parents in any decision they make with regard to Hyo Jin Nim. But we, as leaders of Manhattan Center, humbly request that Hyo Jin Nim not be restored to his position of responsibility here until he has completely overcome his drug and alcohol problems, and can truly uphold God's standard at Manhattan Center and in the movement.

6. True Parents, we ask this in sadness for the burden it reveals to you. But we are united in the conviction that such measures are absolutely necessary for the sake of Hyo Jin Nim's health and well-being and for the continued establishment of True Parents' worldwide foundation.

7. We also wish to express our heartfelt gratitude for Nansook Nim's heart and true leadership in being an absolute link between Manhattan Center and True Parents. She has been tireless in working to bring God's Heart and True Parents' Standard to M.C.

The letter enraged Hyo Jin, which meant trouble for me. Hyo Jin blamed me for the loss of his position. He dragged me into his room. He took a tube of my lipstick and scrawled the word *stupid* all over my face. Another time he threw a bottle of vitamins at me, striking me in the head. Knowing how susceptible I was to the cold after childbirth, he once forced me to stand naked at the foot of his bed while he mocked me. I begged him not to beat me anymore. He gave me a choice. I could be hit or spit upon. I think he enjoyed the humiliation he inflicted by spitting at me even more than he had enjoyed hitting me.

The Reverend and Mrs. Moon had suggested that Hyo Jin and I might help our marriage by living outside the compound. Hyo Jin's reaction had been to remark that the only work I was suited for outside East Garden was prostitution. I knew I could not live with this man, anywhere, under any circumstances. By June I secretly began packing.

My brother called to tell me that there was a house for sale across the street from his in Massachusetts. If I was really serious about fleeing, I would not be alone. I would have family nearby. I cashed in the mutual fund savings I had set aside for the children's college education and what money I had been saving during my time at Manhattan Center.

They had already been where I was going. Two years earlier, Je Jin had made her own final break with the Unification Church and her parents. She came to East Garden to confront her parents with her grievances about the family, and after an ugly scene with her mother, she left the compound and had never come back. The Unification Church describes Je Jin as living apart from the True Family in order for her husband to complete his studies. That is a half-truth. Jin continues to study but Je Jin no longer speaks to her parents or receives any financial support from them.

My parents had left the Unification Church, too. The fact that those closest to me in my own family were now out of harm's way made it easier for me to go. There would be no Hongs left behind to be punished by the Moons for my betrayal.

I did not know where to begin legally. My first impulse was to look under "lawyers" in the Yellow Pages. My brother helped me there, too, steering me to lawyers in New York, where eventually I met Herbert Rosedale, a corporate lawyer in Manhattan whose avocation is helping disenchanted cult members and their families. He was a big, balding, kindly bear of a man, the sixty-three-year-old president of the American Family Foundation, a group of lawyers, business executives, and professionals who try to educate the public about the dangers of religious extremism. I knew I needed someone on my side who would not be intimidated by the Unification Church.

Throughout the summer, I talked with my brother and Madelene about how to arrange my escape. I was frightened that Hyo Jin would stop us if I was open about my plans. He had threatened to kill me so many times, and with a veritable arsenal of weapons in his bedroom, I knew he could. I worried for our safety. I was confirmed in my fears one night in the kitchen of the mansion when Hyo Jin came upon Madelene and me having tea. He told her angrily to leave; he ordered me upstairs. When he joined me, he threatened to break my fingers one by one if I continued to pursue a friendship with her. The next day I went to the police to report his threat.

My parents were very supportive of my plans. We had devoted our lives to a cause that was rotten at its very core. I knew that if I did not leave now, I might not live long enough to make this choice again. I was not going to be beaten, threatened, and imprisoned anymore.

My parents were not aware of the extent of physical danger I was in, but were unwilling to sacrifice another daughter to the church. My younger sister Choong Sook had been matched by the Reverend Moon to a man she did not want to marry, the son of a Blessed Couple my parents did not respect. The Reverend Moon had made that match intentionally to punish my parents for their perceived disloyalty.

Choong Sook was a good daughter; she displayed none of my stubbornness or defiance. A cellist, she was an excellent student at Seoul University. My mother was heartbroken at Choong Sook's fate. She dutifully purchased the wedding garments and gifts for the groom's family, but her heart was heavy. Another daughter was about to walk a lonely and painful path. She couldn't do it. After the religious ceremony, but before Choong Sook and her intended were legally married, my parents sent Choong Sook to America to study. She, too, was in Massachusetts, awaiting my arrival. She would not return to Korea or to the husband the Reverend Moon had selected for her.

All that was left was to ask my children whether they wanted to come with me. If they said no, I knew in my heart I would be unable to leave. How could I abandon the children whose love had kept me strong throughout my painful years with the Moons? How could I risk never seeing them again? How could I doom them to a life inside the Moon compound? I held my breath after I told them my plan. My children exploded in excited, puppylike yelps of pleasure. "We just want to live in a little house with you, Mama," my children told me through their tears.

None of the children revealed our plans to anyone within or outside of the family, even though it meant not being able to say good-bye to their friends and favorite cousins. They knew what was at stake. They had seen the guns in their father's bedroom; they had heard his threats when he beat me.

I picked the day we would leave, but it was God who was guiding my choice. True Parents were out of the country and In Jin and her family were away from East Garden. Baby-sitters whispered about my packing, security guards watched me move furniture out of East Garden, but no one alerted the Moons or their key aides. I was frightened but I knew God was protecting us, clearing a path out of East Garden for my children and me.

My brother called from a motel nearby the night before our scheduled escape to tell me that he would be waiting at our prearranged rendezvous early the next morning. From here on in, he said, it was all up to me. And God, I added.

10

My children had insisted that all they wanted was a little house they could call their own. That's what they got. We moved into a modest split-level in an unpretentious neighborhood of Lexington, Massachusetts, the birthplace of the American Revolution. It seemed like a fitting place to begin my new life. Like the Minuteman whose statue dominates the town green, I, too, had declared my independence from an oppressor.

There is no freedom, though, without security. At my lawyers' urging, the first thing I did when we reached Massachusetts was file a request with the court for an order of protection to prohibit Hyo Jin from having any contact with me. I could imagine his fury when he had awakened and found us gone. I wanted to do what I could to discourage him from trying to find us.

In my affidavit filed with the Massachusetts probate court, I tried to explain that this was not a typical domestic violence case. I was afraid not only of my husband but of the powerful religious cult that sheltered him. Attempts by any member to break away from the Unification Church are fiercely resisted.

What would Sun Myung Moon and his minions do to get his daughter-in-law and five grandchildren back behind the iron gates of East Garden?

The entire legal procedure was intimidating for me, but my fears were eased by the Boston lawyers I had hired with the help of my brother. Ailsa Deitmeyer, an associate in the firm, was especially reassuring, perhaps because she is a woman, perhaps because she is graced with a compassionate heart. She made me feel safe at last.

The court impounded my new address to thwart any efforts by my husband and the Unification Church to contact me. I knew, however, that it was only a matter of time before they learned where I was living. I was a woman with five children, without resources. Where would I go? The Moons eventually would figure out that I had come to my brother; it would not be long before they found me.

I knew that a court order was just a piece of paper, but I thought it might be enough to discourage the Moons from any ideas about taking my children by force. How many custody cases, in circumstances far less bizarre than mine, involve the kidnapping of children?

Standing in the dingy courtroom in Cambridge, I looked past the peeling paint and battered benches. My eyes focused on the American flag. I thanked God I was in America. That flag was protecting me, a Korean girl who had come to this country illegally, who was not yet a citizen. Of all Sun Myung Moon's sins, I thought, his attacks on America were the most vile. He was rich and powerful; I was neither, but we were equal before that flag. The scales would not have been so balanced in my homeland. For me, on that summer day, the United States meant freedom. The stars and stripes were the most beautiful sight I had ever seen.

After helping me unload the cars, Madelene returned immediately to New York and her job at Manhattan Center in order not to arouse suspicion. Hyo Jin had not guessed her role in our escape. He called her every day to ask if she had heard from me. He ordered her to hire a private investigator with Manhattan Center funds to find me, an order she ignored. When I had not returned or contacted Hyo Jin after a few days, the focus of his demands on Madelene changed.

In a telephone conversation that she recorded, Hyo Jin told Madelene to meet him at the corner of 125th Street and Riverside Drive in Harlem with enough money for him to score some crack cocaine. "I just want to numb this feeling, just do the crack. At least when I do it, I can get lost in it. Maddie, I'm sorry, but I have no other choice. I can't deal with these feelings. . . . I don't want to ask anybody else. Come on, Maddie. Do this one for me. Come on. . . . I've got nothing to lose, Madelene. O.K.?"

The next day Madelene drove Hyo Jin to the airport for his trip to a drug treatment program at the Hazelden Clinic in West Palm Beach, Florida. He spent the ride detailing to Madelene the torture he would subject me to if he ever found me. He described graphically how he would peel off my skin and pull out my toenails. I had good reason to be afraid of him.

He lasted at Hazelden only a few days before doctors asked him to leave, citing his lack of cooperation. The Moons sent him next to California to the Betty Ford Clinic, where he remained for more than a month in their detoxification program. It had taken the loss of his wife and children to force Hyo Jin Moon and his parents to address his addiction to alcohol and cocaine. I knew they would expect me to be heartened by this development, but I knew Hyo Jin too well. He would do what he had to do to appease his parents, but I had little faith that whatever level of sobriety he reached in confinement could be sustained once he returned to East Garden.

My children and I, on the other hand, were drunk on our new freedom. Our house was cramped, our sleeping quarters tight, but we were together, out of the shadow of the Moons. The kitchen was especially small, although that was not an immediate concern, since I did not know how to cook. Meal preparation was one of so many domestic chores I had never learned to do. The staff at East Garden had met all of my daily needs for fourteen years. Chefs, launderers, housekeepers, hairdressers, nannies, plumbers, carpenters, auto mechanics, locksmiths, electricians, tailors, gardeners, dentists, doctors, and dozens of security guards were always on call. I did not know how to run a dishwasher, how to mow a lawn, how to operate a washing machine. The first time the toilet over-flowed, I called Madelene in New York in a panic.

It was a difficult adjustment for me, but it was harder still for my children, who had been treated since birth like princes and princesses. It was not easy for children accustomed to maid service to learn to hang up their clothes, to take out the trash, and to clean up their rooms, but they did. They learned to share bedrooms and wait to use our one bathroom. No longer part of the True Family, superior in status to their peers, they adapted to the new egalitarian realities of their lives and began to make friends as equals.

I had neither the money nor the inclination to send them to the kind of private schools they had attended in New York. Tuition for them the previous year had totaled fifty-six thou-sand dollars. If I was going to immerse my children in the real world, what better place to start than the public schools? Lex-ington is a comfortable suburb west of Boston with an excel-lent school system. I was grateful for that.

My children and I stumbled toward self-sufficiency together. We had a lot to learn, but we were not alone. My sister and my brother and his wife helped and supported me. Having them close by meant not feeling afraid as we embarked on this new life. The children had their cousins and I had adults who understood the painful and awkward transition I was trying to make. The worries that disturbed my sleep were not the kind a friendly neighbor could easily relate to over a cup of tea.

I had timed our escape so that it would coincide as closely as possible with the start of the new school year. I knew the children would miss their friends, and I was eager for them to be able to make new ones as soon as possible. In September I enrolled Shin June in seventh grade. She would be the only one of my children at the middle school. She was the oldest and the most independent; I was confident that she would do well academically and socially. The other children would all attend the same neighborhood elementary school. The baby would keep me busy at home.

Their teachers reported few adjustment problems and I saw a house full of happy children. Their father had had so little to do with their lives in New York that it was no surprise to me that they felt only relief that he, as well as all the abuse he represented, was absent from their lives in Massachusetts. Shin June played the flute with a local wind ensemble. Shin Gil made friends easily but was very sensitive to being reprimanded, no matter how gently, by me or a teacher. His teacher reported taking him into the hall once when he seemed tearful to ask what was bothering him. "He told me he used to live in a mansion," she reported. "Now there isn't much privacy and there isn't as much to do. He misses his friends. I asked about his dad. He said that once in a while he misses his dad but that his dad was a drunk who yelled a lot."

Not surprisingly, the first pressure the Moons applied to force us back to East Garden was financial. What savings I had covered our food and basic necessities. My paycheck from Manhattan Center made the difference between being able to pay the monthly mortgage and not. My lawyers had been assured by attorneys for Hyo Jin that those checks would continue to be issued to me until we worked out a temporary child-support arrangement through the probate court.

They weren't. My lawyers filed a formal request with the court for child support. "It appears Ms. Moon's check will be withheld, perhaps trying to force her back into an abusive relationship," my lawyers wrote to church representatives. "Ms. Moon's decision to seek safety from a horrendously dangerous situation was not reached lightly. Having made the decision, however, she is determined not to return, regardless."

With my brother's and sister's help, I had hired Choate, Hall and Stewart, one of Boston's finest firms, to represent me in what I anticipated would be a protracted divorce case. We knew I would need the best lawyers in the city if I was going to take on the Moons. Like so many women facing divorce, I had no idea how I would pay my lawyers. In a study on gender bias in the courts in 1989, the Massachusetts Supreme Judicial Court had concluded that "there is too little legal help available to moderate income women, in part because judges fail to award adequate counsel fees, especially during the pendency of litigation."

My chief lawyers were a brilliant Boston Brahmin named Weld S. Henshaw and his skilled and empathetic associate Ailsa De Prada Deitmeyer. They were confident that the court would require Hyo Jin to pay my legal bills. As experienced as he was, Weld conceded he had never encountered a divorce case quite like mine. Hyo Jin Moon was not the typical defendant; determining his real assets would not be a simple matter.

Hyo Jin retained law firms in New York and Massachusetts, including the Manhattan firm of Levy, Gutman, Goldberg and Kaplan. Gutman was Jeremiah S. Gutman, the former head of the New York Civil Liberties Union, the man who had championed Sun Myung Moon's cause when he was convicted of tax evasion in 1982.

Our case was assigned to Massachusetts probate court judge Edward Ginsburg. He was a fair-minded gentleman, nearing retirement, who ran his Concord probate courtroom in a firm but folksy manner. Something of an eccentric, Judge Ginsburg was easy to spot arriving for work on summer mornings. He was the fellow in the blue seersucker suit with the yappy blond poodle on a leash. His dog, Pumpkin, accompanied the judge to the courthouse every day.

No sooner had I asked the court to require Hyo Jin to support his children than I heard from the Moons directly. Money was a great motivator. In Jin sent a letter through my attorneys to urge me to drop my legal action and come home. She enclosed an audio tape from Mrs. Moon, making the same plea.

It was startling to hear Mrs. Moon's voice in my new surroundings. She could not hide her anger, but she made attempts to sound caring and to be distraught at my departure. The True Family needed to be intact. The bottom line, as always, was that I was at fault. "Nansook, your behavior is not acceptable to all the people who love you." She predicted that I would be condemned by many people in the future and urged me to return ". . . without being changed."

It struck me, as it always had, how selective the Moons could be when applying the teachings of the *Divine Principle*. No one lived her belief in forgiveness more openly than I. Hadn't I forgiven Hyo Jin when he left me for another woman weeks after our wedding? Hadn't I forgiven Hyo Jin when he gave me herpes? Hadn't I forgiven Hyo Jin when he took up with prostitutes? Hadn't I forgiven Hyo Jin when he squandered hundreds of thousands of dollars that had been intended for our children's futures? Hadn't I forgiven Hyo Jin when he beat me and spat upon me? Hadn't I forgiven Hyo Jin when he abandoned me and our children for a life of drug and alcohol abuse? Hadn't I forgiven Hyo Jin when he took a lover on the day I brought our newborn son home from the hospital?

I was not the one who had failed to consider the consequences of my actions. I had spent fourteen years refusing to entertain the idea that I could leave Hyo Jin Moon, that I could make a claim to a life free of fear and violence. I had not left East Garden precipitously. I had tried mightily to make my marriage work. Had the Moons ever thought that it was them, not I, who could be wrong?

In Jin's letter was similar to Mrs. Moon's tape in its judgmental tone. She expressed sympathy for my situation but scoffed at my seeking a restraining order against Hyo Jin, a man who had beaten, humiliated, and threatened me for fourteen years. She accused me of exaggerating the claims in my restraining order that I feared for my life. But her major point was apparently to try and convince me not to use the legal system against the Moons.

She hinted that it would be easy to attribute dark motives to my decision to leave. "Some have even commented that you left your husband after all these years only because he had lost his job and his position in the family," she wrote. I could only convince the family of my good intentions by returning and helping Hyo Jin confront and conquer his alcoholism and drug abuse. "You are hurting everyone who loves you by using the legal system to get what you want," she said, describing the system as "adversarial" and the end result as hurt for everyone.

It was impossible for the Moons to understand that I had already been hurt. I did not want a reconciliation; I wanted release from the abuse of a violent husband and the hold of a religion that had already consumed twenty-nine years of my life. I had never felt a stronger presence of God in my life than at the moment when I decided to flee East Garden. He had lifted the veil from my eyes; I was seeing clearly for the first time. I would never go back.

On October 25, the court ordered Hyo Jin to make monthly support payments for the children and appointed a social worker, Mary Lou Kaufman, to investigate whether visits with their father were in the best interests of our children. I did not want to deprive my children of contact with either their dad or their grandparents. However problematic the relationship, there was no question in my mind that children deserve two parents and two sets of grandparents. I knew that Hyo Jin loved our children, as much as a man as self-absorbed as he could love anyone. However, I urged Ms. Kaufman not to permit visits until the children were more settled and there was demonstrable evidence that Hyo Jin had stopped abusing drugs and alcohol.

I was especially adamant about confirming his sobriety. Hyo Jin prided himself on his ability to circumvent the law. He had once substituted a sample of Shin Gil's urine for his own during a drug test mandated by his drunken driving conviction in New York. It was also noteworthy to me that Hyo Jin had not even asked to see his children until after I applied for financial support.

Ms. Kaufman met Hyo Jin in her office for more than four hours over two days in November. In her report to the court, she noted that he was anxious and highly agitated. He had a dry mouth and was hyperventilating. She suspected he was high on cocaine. He laced his speech with obscenities. He told her that my parents were behind the divorce effort, that my mother had proclaimed herself the Messiah, and that my parents intended to use whatever money I got in a divorce settlement to establish their own church in Korea. He brought my uncle Soon Yoo to support this cockamamy theory. Soon, who had been instrumental in my mother's joining the church, betrayed her to improve his position with the Moons.

Hyo Jin insisted to Ms. Kaufman that he had always been an involved and active father, but he could not tell her the ages of our children or what grades they were in at school. He insisted that if they were not clamoring to see him, it was only because I had poisoned their minds against him. He was shocked to hear that Shin Gil had asked for a picture not of his dad but of one of his toys.

She concluded in her report in early December that no visitation should be allowed between Hyo Jin and the children until Hyo Jin had demonstrated that he had been free of drugs and alcohol for a two-month period.

The children and I were busy preparing for our first Christmas in our new home. My parents were coming from Korea. It had been years since we had all been together. Our reunion would be a celebration of our freedom as well. We decorated the house with the children's drawings from school and a six-foot Christmas tree.

The Saturday before Christmas, I responded to a deliveryman's knock at the front door. My heart raced as I accepted a package with a familiar return address. Hyo Jin had found us. I tried to conceal my concern from my parents and my children, but I had become less adept at disguising my emotions since leaving the Moon compound. The package contained several small Christmas gifts for the children and a card addressed to me in Korean. In it, Hyo Jin alluded to my revelations about his substance-abuse problems in court documents and asked how I would feel if my own "nakedness" were exposed to the world. It was a veiled threat to expose a videotape he had made of me in the nude.

My father, noticing my distress, tried to comfort me. "Don't let him get to you," my father advised. "If you're down, he's succeeded in his goal to hurt you." He was right. I had done nothing wrong. Hyo Jin had. His letter was a criminal violation of the restraining order that prohibited him from contacting me. The son of Sun Myung Moon still thought he was above the law. I reported the threat to the police. Hyo Jin was charged with a criminal offense.

Through my attorneys, Hyo Jin sent letters to the children, expressing his love for them and his desire to see them. He could not resist criticizing me, however. In his letter to Shin June, he wrote: "Of course I feel angry at times at your mother but I want to forgive her. There are a lot of things you don't know about your mother but that's not important. You know why? It is because I want you to be a loving person who can love someone forever and not give up on the person that you love and also learn to forgive them as they face trials that life will offer, as it offers to everyone."

To Shin Ok he wrote that he knew she loved him. "If there was no one telling you how bad Dad is I truly think you would never think even for the moment that way. You know what? Even if you think Dad is bad I feel OK because I won't be bad any more."

He promised all the children that he would write to them again soon but he never did.

In February 1996 Hyo Jin met again with Ms. Kaufman to assess the wisdom of allowing visits with the children. He was outraged that he had been barred from seeing them for so long. He talked about the revenge he would seek against me in court.

He told Ms. Kaufman he would hire "a cutthroat legal firm from New York" to ruin me financially. He was attending meetings of Alcoholics Anonymous, he said, and was now committed to a life of sobriety.

Ms. Kaufman granted supervised visits with the children that spring. Hyo Jin saw his children only twice before the man who insisted he had changed forever failed a drug test. Visits were suspended until Hyo Jin could prove to the court's satisfaction that he was no longer abusing drugs or alcohol. That day still has not come.

For all his accusations of being denied contact with his children, Hyo Jin has made no effort to stay in touch with them. His letters, to be delivered through my attorneys, were encouraged by the court, but he never wrote to them. He does not send them cards or gifts on their birthdays or at Christmas. He does not inquire how they are doing in school.

As troubling as their memories of their father are, his abandonment of them is painful for our children. Shin Gil, the favored son now living on my limited income, especially remembers how his father indulged him at video arcades and with expensive toys. Shin Hoon, the baby who never knew his father, wonders where he is. When I take him to nursery school, he often asks, "When is my daddy going to pick me up like the other kids'?"

Divorce is never easy for children, but for a man who claims to be part of the True Family, the embodiment of traditional moral values, Hyo Jin Moon has made it much more difficult for our children than it needed to be.

The Moons did not always pay the court-ordered child support. When they did, the check always came late and only after reminders from my lawyers, who were billing me for more hours than I could ever hope to pay. I had to sell some of my jewelry one month to pay routine expenses. Hyo Jin's position was that he could not pay my legal bills because he had no source of income. He had been fired from Manhattan Center and cut off from the True Family Trust. He asked the court to believe that the son of one of the wealthiest men in the world was destitute.

Judge Ginsburg was not buying it. The lines between Unification Church funds and Moon family money and Hyo Jin Moon's finances were imaginary. Hyo Jin had access to limitless funds while reporting few assets and only modest income. In terms of housing, travel, cars, private schools, and servants, he and his siblings lived without any budgetary constraint. For Hyo Jin to argue that he had no money because he was unemployed was to ignore the fact that his employment at Manhattan Center Studios had been no more independent of his father than his living arrangements. His father housed him, fed him, and employed him. Take away the Unification Church and the uneducated Hyo Jin Moon was unemployable. It was laughable to suggest that whatever assets he had, and he claimed he had few, had been acquired in any way other than through the largesse of Sun Myung Moon.

To maintain the fiction that Hyo Jin was destitute, one had to ignore that all his income led back to the same source: Sun Myung Moon. Noting the fine cut of the suits being worn by the army of attorneys from Boston and New York who accompanied Hyo Jin Moon to court, Judge Ginsburg ordered him to pay my counsel fees or face arrest for contempt of court.

The Moons would not pay. That summer Sun Myung Moon sponsored an international conference in Washington, D.C., to discuss how to restore traditional family values. The irony was almost too rich. Hyo Jin Moon could not attend the two-day symposium in the Great Hall of the National Building Museum to hear speakers such as former presidents Gerald Ford and George Bush, former British prime minister Edward

Heath, former Costa Rican president and Nobel Peace Prize winner Oscar Arias, and Republican presidential hopeful Jack Kemp address the erosion of family values around the world. Sun Myung Moon's son was languishing in a Massachusetts jail cell, where Judge Ginsburg had sent him for defying his order to pay my legal bills. He would remain there for three months, winning his release only after he formally filed for bankruptcy in New York State to prove that he was a man without financial resources.

Money became a constant source of worry for me. What if the Moons did not send the check? What if my lawyers got tired of waiting to be paid? How would I care for my children? I had an undergraduate degree in art history. I wasn't qualified to do anything more than volunteer as a tour guide at the Boston Museum of Fine Arts. That would not pay the dental bills for five children. In my desperation, I applied for a sales position at Macy's department store at the local shopping mall. I completed the training course by asking my sister and Madelene to baby-sit. Madelene had left the church one month after I did and moved close by. I could not have gotten through my first year of freedom without her and my sister and brother. Only when I was trained did I learn that Macy's expected me to work every weekend. How could I? Who would watch my children? I returned home, feeling defeated.

Independence has its price. I needed to settle my divorce case and move on with my life. I would need more education if I was going to land a job that would allow me to give my children the advantages they deserved, advantages their cousins in East Garden took for granted.

Through my attorneys, I proposed a divorce settlement that would sever my ties forever to the family of Sun Myung Moon. I asked that trust funds be established for me and for my children from which I would pay for our health insurance, education, clothing, housing, and all other expenses. There would be no alimony and no child support. I would pay my own legal fees. My lawyers summarized my intentions in the proposal: "The concept of a trust such as this would insure there was no likelihood of these assets being dissipated so that the settlement could truly be finished now and forever with no second chances."

Sun Myung Moon refused. He was firm that Hyo Jin's financial situation was independent from his own. He would not take responsibility for the future well-being of his grandchildren. In addition, the Moons demanded that the terms of any divorce agreement remain confidential. They did not want me to talk. I refused all demands for confidentiality.

In a deposition filed with the court in July 1997, Sun Myung Moon made his position clear.

> *When my son, Hyo Jin Moon, was cut off as a beneficiary of the True Family Trust and was discharged from his position as an employee, officer and director of Manhattan Center Studios, Inc. and was subsequently discontinued from his status as a disabled employee receiving disability payments from Manhattan Center Studios, Inc. my concern and love for his five children, my grandchildren, moved me to provide support funds fixed by order of the court in Massachusetts having jurisdiction of the dispute between my son and his wife.*
>
> *My son, Hyo Jin Moon, had and has no control over whether I choose each month to make and continue to make such payments. They are voluntarily made by me so long as I am able and willing to do so.*
>
> *Negotiations have broken down and I now learn that my daughter-in-law is making efforts to re-incarcerate my son, despite the fact that he has no assets or income*

other than a $3,500 gross salary per month from his
re-employment by Manhattan Center Studios, Inc. I am
re-thinking the situation.

The implied threat, that if I did not settle on the Moons' terms, child support payments would be cut off, was not subtle. The Reverend Moon paid fifty thousand dollars toward my counsel fees to keep his son out of jail, not out of respect for the court that ordered the bills paid.

"I am pleased that Hyo Jin Moon has recovered sufficiently to resume his productivity as a producer of musical recordings and I hope he will be able to continue to be artistically creative and productive and to earn sufficiently so that I can discontinue supporting him as I have consistently done since he was cut off from all income," the Reverend Moon said, still ignoring the reality that Hyo Jin's job only existed because his father created it.

Our divorce case had produced enough paper to make a stack of legal documents two feet high. It had dragged on for two and one-half years. Sun Myung Moon had displayed more willingness to pay hundreds of thousands of dollars to lawyers than to guarantee the future security of his grandchildren. So much for family values.

In December 1997 I settled for a token lump sum payment and a continuation of monthly child support. If we were dependent on monthly support payments, I knew we would forever be at the mercy of the Moons. Once the litigation had ended, Sun Myung Moon could cut off the money at any time. I could not imagine a more likely candidate for a "deadbeat Dad" than Hyo Jin Moon.

Still, I wanted this to be over. I was tired. My attorneys had fought hard and done the best they could for me. I could not have asked for better counsel. How many other women in protracted divorce fights felt just as I did: he with the most resources wins? There would be no alimony, no compensation for the fourteen lost years of my life. There would be no trust fund to ensure that my children had access to a college education. If the children wanted money for schooling, Hyo Jin's attorneys told my own, they would have to come to Sun Myung Moon personally and ask their grandfather.

I did not oppose supervised visitation by Sun Myung Moon and Hak Ja Han Moon, but I was skeptical that they were sincere in this demand. In the two and one-half years that had passed since we fled East Garden, they had not written or called their grandchildren once. They had not remembered them at Christmas or on their birthdays. They had displayed the same indifference to them as had their son.

At 9:15 A.M. on a cold, sunny December morning, I stood across from Hyo Jin Moon in the well of a small courtroom in Concord, Massachusetts. I answered, "Yes, Your Honor," when Judge Edward Ginsburg asked me if my marriage was beyond saving. Hyo Jin mumbled a disrespectful "Yeah" when asked the same question. Judge Ginsburg reminded us, as he did all divorcing couples, that marriages end but parenthood does not. He granted my request to legally restore my maiden name, and with the flick of a judge's pen, the nightmare that was my marriage to the abusive son of a false Messiah was over at last.

No one had really won. Not me. Not Hyo Jin. Not our children. Only Sun Myung Moon had gotten what he wanted all along. My children and I had slipped out of the grasp of the Unification Church, but we were destined to remain in the shadow of the Moons.

Epilogue

The Messiah is seventy-eight years old. His claims of divinity notwithstanding, even Sun Myung Moon cannot live forever. When he dies there is every possibility that the Reverend Moon will take the Unification Church with him to his grave.

The Reverend Moon has made no concrete plans for his succession. To do so would require him to relinquish some power while he is still alive, and that prospect is inconceivable to a man accustomed to being the central figure in a tightly controlled universe. The Unification Church is a classic example of what psychologists call a cult of personality.

The failure to designate and groom a successor all but guarantees a familial bloodletting after the Reverend Moon's death. His sons are already locked in a battle for control of his business empire. That struggle will only intensify when the Unification Church itself is up for grabs.

Leadership, of course, should fall naturally to the eldest son, but given Hyo Jin's continuing problems with alcohol and drugs, his brothers are already jockeying for position. Even In Jin, who has no chance to succeed her father because she is a woman, is desperate to salvage Hyo Jin's candidacy. She cast her lot with him a long time ago. If he goes down, she and Jin Sung Pak go down with him.

When he addresses the issue at all these days, the Reverend Moon implies that the True Mother will rule when he ascends into Heaven. No one in the church seriously believes that Hak Ja Han Moon is either capable of taking or inclined to take any more than a symbolic role at the helm of the Unification Church.

A month before I left East Garden, Mrs. Moon and I spoke about the future of the Unification Church. I urged her not to turn control over to Hyo Jin. I could not imagine a more unstable individual to lead a nominally religious enterprise. She reluctantly agreed that Sun Myung Moon might have to look to one of his other sons to lead the Unification Church. I know that possibility saddened her. Hyo Jin's birth, after her first child was a daughter, had sealed her position as the True Mother. Her fate and his had seemed bound together.

The evil at the heart of the Unification Church is the hypocrisy and deceit of the Moons, a family that is all too human in its incredible level of dysfunction. To continue to promote the myth that the Moons are spiritually superior to the idealistic young people who are drawn to the church is a shameful deceit. Hyo Jin's failings may be more conspicuous, but there is not a member of the second generation of Moons to whom the word *pious* could fairly be applied.

Sun Myung Moon wrote the epitaph for the Unification Church in a sermon in 1984 about the moral and spiritual decline of the United States. His words could better be applied to his own family. "Sodom and Gomorrah were destroyed by God's judgment for the immorality and pursuit of luxury. Rome was in the same situation. It did not collapse from external invasion but from the weight of its own corruption."

The Unification Church still claims millions of members worldwide. How many of those are active fund-raisers and participants in church affairs is another question. Unlike other religions, the Unification Church has few formal worship sites where attendance could be taken. Some cities have churches, others don't.

Even many of the church training centers, where religious services and seminars were held, closed in the early 1990s during Sun Myung Moon's disastrous experiment called home church. In response to the negative publicity about the public proselytizing of the Moonies, the Reverend Moon sent members home to convert their relatives and neighbors. Such decentralization, however, weakened the control the Reverend Moon maintained over his flock. Many members, reexposed to the wider world and their families' disapproval of Sun Myung Moon, just drifted away.

In the wake of that failure, the Reverend Moon and church leaders regrouped. In the last few years, they have orchestrated a remarkably successful campaign to win respectability and wield political influence. As usual, they have succeeded by deceitful means. The Unification Church has launched dozens of civic organizations around the world dedicated to women's rights, world peace, and family values that have made impressive inroads into mainstream society. None of them advertise their relationship with Sun Myung Moon or the Unification Church.

The Women's Federation for World Peace, the Family Federation for World Peace, the International Cultural Foundation, the Professors World Peace Academy, the Washington Institute for Values in Public Policy, the Summit Council for World Peace, the American Constitution Committee, and dozens of other organizations present themselves as nonpartisan, nondenominational groups. All of them are funded by Sun Myung Moon.

In March 1994 for instance, the Women's Federation for World Peace sponsored a program "promoting peace and reconciliation" at the State University of New York campus in Purchase. Hyun Jin Moon, the Reverend Moon's then twenty-five-year-old son, opened the event with a declaration that Sun Myung Moon had a new divine revelation for America. The organization had solicited a welcoming letter from Sandra Galef, the local state assemblywoman. She was never told the group was affiliated with Sun Myung Moon.

"I have never supported the Unification Church," the angry assemblywoman later told the *New York Times*. "I have always felt they are a group that destroys families. If the individual who came into my office requesting a letter had honestly told me what this organization was, I never would have given it to them. Basically it was a hoax."

The same month, the Toronto chapter of Women's Federation for World Peace and the University of Toronto branch of CARP cosponsored an AIDS-prevention program for teenagers at North York Public Library. The promotional flyer invited parents to enroll their children to ensure that they "choose a lifestyle without disease and drugs." Nowhere did it mention the Unification Church or Sun Myung Moon.

Some of the biggest celebrities in the United States have been seduced by exorbitant speaking fees to participate in programs sponsored by these groups without ever knowing their affiliation with the Moonies. Gerald Ford, the former president; Barbara Walters, the television journalist; Christopher Reeve, the actor; Sally Ride, the first American woman in space; Coretta Scott King, the civil rights leader; and Bill Cosby, the comedian, have all spoken at functions sponsored by the Women's Federation for World Peace.

Perhaps the worst offenders have been former president George Bush and Barbara Bush. They do know the relationship between the Reverend Moon and these groups, and yet they were reportedly paid more than a million dollars in 1995 to address six rallies in Japan sponsored by the Women's Federation for World Peace.

The former president is not naive. Certainly George Bush knows that when he hails Sun Myung Moon as "a visionary," as he did in a speech in Buenos Aires in 1996, he is legitimizing the work of a man who uses manipulation and deceit to recruit cheap labor to work to finance his lavish lifestyle. President Bush was paid to attend a party with the Reverend Moon in Buenos Aires to launch *Tiempos del Mundo,* or the *Times of the World,* an eighty-page weekly Spanish-language tabloid newspaper distributed to seventeen countries in South America.

Every photograph of the Reverend Moon with a world political leader enhances his credibility. Pictures of Sun Myung Moon as an international religious leader get politicians like Argentina's President Carlos Saul Menem to meet with him when he has no more than a few thousand followers in that country.

What influence the Reverend Moon does not wield through his political connections, he exercises through his financial investments in real estate, banking, and media. In Latin America alone, those holdings are valued at hundreds of millions of dollars.

Mainstream religious leaders in the heavily Catholic region have proved less than receptive to Sun Myung Moon's recruitment efforts. "Deceptive proselytizing by institutions like the Unification Church are hurting the good faith of Christians of our country and other countries across Latin America," a group of Catholic bishops in Uruguay said in a statement issued in 1996. "These organizations promote fundamental human values, but in reality they attempt to convert believers to their religious movement."

The Unification Church's biggest challenge in the years ahead will be holding on to Japan as the financial engine that runs this moneymaking machine. For decades Japan has been Sun Myung Moon's strongest base of support and most reliable source of cash. However, fund-raising efforts there have begun to stall in the last few years in the wake of public complaints, lawsuits, and government scrutiny of church operations. The church claims to have 460,000 members in Japan, but critics say the figure is closer to 30,000, and that only 10,000 of those are active members.

The Reverend Moon founded the *Washington Times* in 1982 to counter what he charged was the liberal bias of the American press, especially the *Washington Post*. The Washington Times Corporation also publishes a weekly newsmagazine called *Insight,* also founded to parrot the Reverend Moon's anti-Communist ideology. His timing was perfect; the *Washington Times* became a favorite publication of the conservative Republican president Ronald Reagan. Key Reagan administration officials often leaked information to its reporters. Although editors claim that both publications are independent of the Unification Church, the first editor and publisher of the *Washington Times,* James Whelan, was fired after he objected to the church's interference.

With its marble columns, brass railings, and plush carpeting, the *Washington Times* headquarters looks like a more profitable operation than it is. The paper continues to lose money sixteen years after the first press run. It is subsidized by the profits of the Reverend Moon's other business holdings and, increasingly, by "donations" from Japanese members.

At a dinner celebrating the tenth anniversary of the *Washington Times* in 1992, the Reverend Moon said he had invested close to a billion dollars in the paper in its first decade in order to make it "an instrument to save America and the world." The Reverend

Moon told the crowd at the Omni Shoreham Hotel in Washington that he founded the *Times* because "I believed it was the will of God" to have him run a newspaper with a mission of "saving the world from the collapse of traditional values, and to defend the free world from the threat of communism."

That was the same year the Reverend Moon rescued the University of Bridgeport from bankruptcy, providing the Unification Church with a legitimate academic institution from which to mount its efforts to save the world. The Professors World Peace Academy, a Moonie front, has spent more than a hundred million dollars to keep the Connecticut university afloat. A group calling itself the Coalition of Concerned Citizens had opposed the Reverend Moon's offer to bail out the university in exchange for a controlling number of seats on the board of trustees. The university community voted for survival. In the end, professors' fears about the influence of the Moons on academic freedom were overwhelmed by their desire to save their jobs.

Trustees were willing to overlook the real source of the bailout to save their school, blithely accepting Sun Myung Moon's assurances that the Unification Church itself would have no contact with the university. In 1997 the Unification Church made explicit its relationship with the University of Bridgeport by opening a boarding school on campus. New Eden Academy International serves forty-four high-school-age children of church members. Its headmaster is Hugh Spurgin, who has been a follower of Sun Myung Moon for twenty-nine years. His wife is the president of the Women's Federation for World Peace, another Moonie front. University classrooms are being used by the high school for a full array of classes, including religious training. The students eat in the university's dining halls and study in its library, but the boarding school still insists it is independent and merely renting space on campus.

City councilman William Finch, a leader of the Coalition of Concerned Citizens, was right when he told the *New York Times:* "It shows just how far the Unification Church has come in its efforts to be accepted by mainstream society, because nobody seems to care, or be bothered by this."

Plenty of people are bothered by the Unification Church in Japan, however. Hundreds have sued, charging they were cheated out of their life savings by Unification Church members who promised that Sun Myung Moon's intercession could save a deceased loved one from the fires of hell. Government consumer protection officials in Japan say they have received nearly twenty thousand complaints about the Unification Church since 1987. The church already has paid out millions to settle many of the lawsuits involving the sale of vases, icons, and paintings said to have supernatural powers.

The Unification Church has never had much religious appeal in the United States or in Europe. Its business holdings are extensive and the wealth generated by those enterprises is enormous. As a spiritual entity, however, the Unification Church has been something of a bust. The church claims to have fifty thousand members in the United States, but I would put the number of active members at no more than a few thousand in the United States and no more than a few hundred in England. Sun Myung Moon himself was banned from Britain in 1995 because the Home Office, which is in charge of immigration, declared his presence was "not conducive to the public good." It isn't as easy as it used to be to find impressionable young people willing to spend eighteen hours a day selling novelty items out of the back of a van to raise money for the Messiah.

The Reverend Moon hoped to find those recruits among the ranks of his old enemies, the Communists. In 1990 the Unification Church began a major recruitment and investment drive in the Soviet Union. Sun Myung Moon met in the Kremlin with President Mikhail Gorbachev and also invited a select group of Soviet journalists to his home in Seoul for his first interview in ten years. That same year, Bo Hi Pak, one of Moon's top aides, led a delegation of businessmen from Korea, Japan, and the United States to Moscow to explore investment opportunities. Before leaving, Bo Hi Pak wrote a one hundred thousand dollar check to one of Raisa Gorbachev's favorite cultural foundations.

The Reverend Moon's efforts in Russia seemed to stall after the collapse of Communism and the breakup of the Soviet Union. His false start there was overshadowed by his disastrous investment in China. At the urging of Bo Hi Pak, the Reverend Moon invested $250 million to build an automobile plant in Huizhou in southern China. He promised to invest a billion dollars in Panda Motors Corporation to blanket the country with subcompact cars. The Reverend Moon claimed his goal was not to make a profit but to invest in poorer nations. His commitment to the development of mainland China disappeared when bureaucratic obstacles and poor planning slowed down progress on the plant. He soon abandoned the project and redoubled his efforts in South America, where church leaders think the future is brighter.

I have begun taking courses at the University of Massachusetts while my children are in school. I am studying psychology, perhaps motivated as much by a need to understand what happened to me as to prepare for a career helping others in emotional distress. I was a battered woman, but I was also part of a religious cult. I am in the process of trying to understand the decisions I did and did not make over the course of fourteen years.

One thing I have learned from experience: the mind is a complicated thing. Words like *brainwashing* and *mind control* are better suited to political than psychological discussions of the Unification Church. Catchphrases cannot fully explain the attraction of groups like the Moonies or the hold they have on their followers.

If I believed I had been brainwashed, I could escape the depression and self-flagellation that have accompanied my new freedom. I do not yet fully understand how I remained blind for so long to the charlatan in Sun Myung Moon. My experience was different from that of recruited members. I was not deprived of sleep or food, subjected to hours of indoctrinating lectures, or separated from my family. I was born into this religion. My parents were steeped in the traditions and beliefs of a church that dictated where they lived, what work they did, and with whom they associated. I knew nothing else.

I feel duped, but I do not feel bitter. I feel used, but I feel more sad than angry. I long to have the years back that I lost to Sun Myung Moon. I wish I could be a girl again. I wonder if I will ever know romantic love, if I will ever trust a man or any so-called leader again.

In many ways I am a thirty-year-old woman experiencing a delayed adolescence. I am learning along with my fifteen-year-old daughter about independence, rebellion, fashion, peer pressure, personal responsibility. I am sometimes overwhelmed by my responsibilities, but I savor the freedom I now have to make my own choices. I am in control of my life. There is no more liberating feeling in the world. For the first time, I have a sense of real happiness. I have a renewed sense of energy as I pursue my studies and my volunteer work at a shelter for battered women. I have discovered with satisfaction that I have a contribution to make to my community, as well as to my children.

There is an old Korean proverb: Blame yourself, not the river, if you fall into the water. For the first time in my life, that dictum makes sense to me. I, alone, am in charge of my life. I, alone, am responsible for my actions and for the decisions I make. It is terrifying. I spent half of my lifetime ceding all decisions to a "higher authority." Learning to make decisions for myself means being willing to accept the consequences — the bad ones as well as the good ones.

I spend a lot of time explaining that principle to my children these days. I know the time could come when one of them will tell me that he or she wants to go back to the Unification Church. As Hyo Jin Moon's eldest son, Shin Gil, I know, will one day be subjected to enormous pressure to return. On the jacket cover of the latest compact disc by his new band, the Apocalypse, Hyo Jin has used a photograph of himself with Shin Gil. The title of the album is *Hold on to Your Love*.

I pray that neither Shin Gil nor any of his siblings will be lured back to East Garden as adults. If they are, I will be saddened but accepting. I hope I will have taught them to make thoughtful, informed choices. I hope I will have taught them not to be swayed by the temptation of money or the illusion of power. I hope I will have taught them that we all must work for what we want in life; that unless we earn something, it is not really ours; that if something seems too good to be true, it probably is.

I will always love my children, no matter what their choices, just as I have always loved my parents, no matter my regret about some of theirs. I hope my relationship with my children will always be open and honest enough to allow us to disagree without those disagreements coming between us. That is real love, not marching in lockstep behind any Messiah.

I admit to some cynicism these days about organized religion. Those who see dangers only in "cults" ignore how fine the line is between the religious mainstream and the religious extreme. What really distinguishes those who believe that Sun Myung Moon is the Messiah from those who believe that the pope is infallible? What religion does not claim that it alone knows the best path to Heaven? Many faiths demand some suspension of critical thinking. The difference, of course, is that legitimate religions encourage believers to come freely to belief. There are no deceptive recruitment practices, no economic exploitation, no forced isolation from the rest of the world.

I have become disillusioned about religion, but not about God. I still believe in a Supreme Being. I believe that it was God who opened my eyes and God who gave me both the strength to survive and the courage to flee. My God is an all-embracing deity who supports me through my most painful struggles. He was at my side when I was a child bride, when I was a teenage mother, when I was a battered wife. He is with me now as I work to raise my children in his image. People of faith call God by different names, depict him in different ways, but we all know his heart. The God I trust gave me the ability to think; he expects me to use it.

On November 29, 1997, Sun Myung Moon presided over a mass wedding at Robert F. Kennedy Stadium in Washington, D.C. It was a far cry from a similar event in Madison Square Garden in 1982. For this latest gathering, the Unification Church had to beat the bushes to fill the stadium. Most of the twenty-eight thousand couples who attended were already married and members of other religions. Many had accepted free tickets passed out at suburban shopping malls and in supermarket parking lots to attend what the Unification Church billed as a "World Culture and Sports Festival." The lure was not Sun Myung Moon, the Messiah. It was Whitney Houston, the pop singer. She had been offered one million dollars to sing for forty-five minutes. Unfortunately for those who came to hear her, after Houston learned just days before the event of Sun Myung Moon's sponsorship, she canceled, citing sudden illness.

She was not the only celebrity who begged off. Pakistani prime minister Benazir Bhutto, Christian Coalition leader Ralph Reed, Camelia Anwar Sadat, daughter of the assassinated Egyptian president, all changed their plans to attend after learning that the festival was a publicity stunt by Sun Myung Moon.

When the Unification Church realized it could not hide its association with the festival, Sun Myung Moon took out full-page newspaper advertisements inviting married couples to attend an "ecumenical" event designed to renew their wedding vows and strengthen family values. "You may think of me as a man surrounded by controversy," the Reverend Moon's ad read. "We are not trying to promote me as an individual or expand the Unification Church as an institution. Our goal is to bring together all peoples and all religions in an effort to strengthen families."

Of those in attendance at RFK Stadium on that chilly autumn afternoon, only a few hundred were newly matched couples in the Unification Church. Sun Myung Moon's two youngest sons were among them. They had actually been married a few months before. At the lavish family banquet that followed their double wedding, the head table was set with place cards for every member of the True Family. The Moons were determined to maintain the public fiction of family unity and perfection. There was a place setting for Je Jin and another for Jin, though Sun Myung Moon's oldest daughter and my brother were at home in Massachusetts with their children.

There was a place card bearing my name on the head table alongside the one for Hyo Jin Moon. My chair was empty, as if I had just stepped away from the table and the True Family expected me to return at any moment.